THE CENTURY PSYCHOLOGY SERIES
Richard M. Elliott, *Editor*

The Cultural Background
of Personality

The Cultural Background of Personality

by

RALPH LINTON
Professor of Anthropology
Columbia University

HM
107
L5

APPLETON-CENTURY-CROFTS, INC.

NEW YORK

68162

COPYRIGHT, 1945, BY
D. APPLETON–CENTURY COMPANY, INC.

All rights reserved. This book, or parts thereof, must not be reproduced in any form without permission of the publisher.

620-9

PRINTED IN THE UNITED STATES OF AMERICA

Good Background
Book on Culture
& Personality
Formation

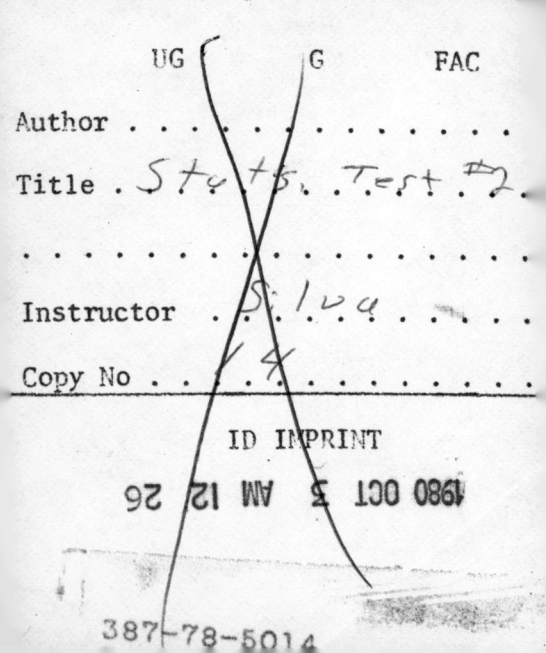

TO

THE STUDENTS

WHOSE QUESTIONS MAY INDUCE THEIR PROFESSORS
TO READ THIS BOOK

Preface

IN February, 1943, Swarthmore College invited me to deliver a series of five lectures on the general subject of the interrelations of Culture, Society and the Individual, these lectures being given under the auspices of the Cooper Foundation. As an alumnus of the institution and one who had had few opportunities to revisit it since graduation in 1915, it gave me great pleasure to accept. My stay at Swarthmore was an exceedingly pleasant one, and I wish to thank President John W. Nason and Dr. Charles B. Shaw for the invitation which made my visit possible and for their many kindnesses during the time that I was in residence at the college. I also wish to express my appreciation for the many pleasant contacts which I had with various members of the faculty. I was especially happy to renew my acquaintance with Dr. Harold C. Goddard and Dr. Samuel Palmer, both of whom had contributed greatly to my education as well as my instruction in the days when I was an undergraduate.

In the course of preparing my lecture notes I became keenly conscious of two things: the complexity of the problems involved and the necessity for a clearer exposition of certain of the concepts which it was necessary to employ in dealing with these problems. I was still more impressed with these when I came to prepare the lectures for publication. After various attempts to adhere to my original outline, it seemed that a thorough revision would be necessary to make the material of any value. As a result, the five essays included in the present volume differ considerably from the original lectures in both form and content. They represent the lectures as they should have been delivered, not as they were delivered.

In the preparation of these essays I received substantial assistance from certain members of the Department of Anthropology of Yale University whom the fortunes of war had placed temporarily at Columbia University. Dr. George P. Murdock, Dr. John M. Whiting, and Dr. Clellan S. Ford all read the various essays as they were completed and made many valuable suggestions. I am also indebted to Dr. A. H. Maslow for a thorough and painstaking critique of the entire manuscript, and to Dr. Abram Kardiner for numerous suggestions on points involving psychoanalytic theory. Last but not least, I wish to thank Miss Ruth W. Bryan, Secretary of the Department at Columbia, for her invaluable assistance in preparing the manuscript for publication.

R. L.

Contents

	PAGE
PREFACE	vii
INTRODUCTION	xiii

CHAPTER
1. THE INDIVIDUAL, CULTURE AND SOCIETY . . . 1
2. THE CONCEPT OF CULTURE 27
3. SOCIAL STRUCTURE AND CULTURE PARTICIPATION . 55
4. PERSONALITY 83
5. THE RÔLE OF CULTURE IN PERSONALITY FORMATION 125
INDEX 155

The Cultural Background
of Personality

Introduction

THE most recent development in man's long effort to understand himself is the systematic study of the interrelations of the individual, society and culture. This study lies at the meeting point of three long-established scientific disciplines: Psychology, Sociology and Anthropology. Each of these disciplines has elected to deal with a particular series of phenomena, has developed its own techniques and can show a fine record of accomplishment. However, it is becoming increasingly evident that there are certain problems which cannot be solved by any one discipline alone. The term *certain problems* is used advisedly since each discipline covers a wide area and deals with problems of several different sorts and magnitudes. Certain of these can be dealt with quite adequately without collaboration across disciplinary lines. Thus the Experimental Psychologist working with animals can go his own way with little reference to the findings of Sociology and Anthropology. These become important only when he tries to apply his own findings to the understanding of human behavior. Again, the Social Worker, confronted by concrete problems which must be solved within the frame of our own society and culture, needs little help from the Anthropologist. At the same time, he is beginning to lean on the Psychologist and the indications are that he will do so increasingly as time goes on. Lastly, within the wide and diffuse field of Anthropological studies, the Archaeologist or Physical Anthropologist can answer many specific questions without taking council with either Psychologists or Sociologists. It is the workers in the fields of Personality Psychology, Social Structure, and Cultural Anthropology who find themselves drawn together by common interests.

Out of the collaboration of such workers there is beginning to emerge a new science devoted to the dynamics of human behavior. This science is still in the first stages of its development, but it is characterized by a willingness to follow problems without reference to disciplinary boundaries and to use any data or techniques which seem germane to the research in hand. Its practitioners have, for the most part, received formal training in only one of the established disciplines and often find it difficult to deal with the materials provided by the others. They also tend to be most conscious of problems which have originated within their original discipline. Thus investigators who, like the present writer, have been drawn into the new area from Anthropology, are most keenly aware of the implications of the new approach for the understanding of cultural problems. The Anthropologists' studies of culture process and culture integration have now reached a point where further progress necessitates the use of the findings of Personality Psychology. Every culture is participated in, perpetuated and modified by a particular society but every society is, in the last analysis, a group of individuals. These individuals constitute the unsolved X in every cultural equation and an X which cannot be solved by purely Anthropological techniques. Although Anthropologists have long since abandoned the "Great Man" theory of the early Historians, they know that there can be no inventions without inventors. They also know that there can be no lasting modifications in culture without the acceptance of new ideas by a society's members. The next step is to discover what makes a man an inventor rather than a passive culture carrier and why the members of a particular society are ready to accept one innovation or to reject another. As applied to the development of cultures, the convenient phrase "historic accident" is only a screen for ignorance; a magic word which serves to lull the curiosity. There are many cases in which the activities of the inventor cannot be related to the obvious, conscious needs of his society. Similarly, a society's acceptance or rejection of a new thing very often cannot be explained in the simple, mechanistic terms of culture integration. To understand these things we must turn to the findings of Psychology. It seems highly probable that the phenomena of acceptance and rejection are related in some way to the congeniality of the new thing with the personality norm of the society's members. The application of the techniques of Personality Psychology to the study of societies and cultures has already enabled investigators to recognize that there are differences in these norms and to gain some insight into the factors responsible for such differences. When these investigations have been completed, we may anticipate that the particular directions which various cultures have taken in their development will no longer appear accidental.

If the Anthropologist can profit from collaboration with the Personality Psychologist, he can at least offer a fair exchange of aid. The most fundamental problem which confronts students of personality today is that of the degree to which the deeper levels of personality are conditioned by environmental factors. This problem cannot be solved by laboratory techniques. It is impossible to create controlled environments comparable to the social-cultural configurations within which all human beings develop. Neither can one appraise the influence of many environmental factors by observations carried on within the frame of our own culture and society. Many of the factors operative here are taken so much for granted that they never enter into the investigator's calculations. The only way in which the Personality Psychologist can get the comparative data which he requires is by the study of individuals reared in different societies and cultures. Under present conditions he rarely has the opportunity to make such studies at first hand, but he can obtain much of the information which he needs from the material which has been or can be collected by Anthropologists. The so called "primitive" societies which Anthropologists have made their special field of investigation presents a variety of social-cultural environments sufficiently great to provide answers to most of the Psychologist's questions. Moreover, in their studies of culture the Anthropologists have developed effective techniques for summarizing this environmental material and showing the experiences to which the bulk of any society's members are subjected in the course of their lives. Unfortunately, the information which Anthropologists can provide on the personalities of individuals reared in these varying environments is still far from satisfactory. However, their sins in this respect tend to be those of omission rather than of commission. They frequently fail to record data which would be of great interest to the Psychologist simply because they do not realize that such data are important.

Since the present volume deals primarily with problems which are of interest mainly to the Psychologist and Anthropologist, the rôle of Sociology in the development of the new science of human behavior can be passed over lightly. Suffice it to say that the interpersonal relations which are of such paramount importance in the formation of personality cannot be understood except with reference to the positions which the individuals involved occupy in the structural system of their society. It is also impossible to understand or delimit the individual's culturally ascribed rights and obligations without taking this system into account. Conversely, the structure of any society is itself a part of the society's culture and many of its features cannot be understood except in relation to the organization of that culture as a whole. Sociology has as much to gain and as important contributions to make in collaboration as have either of the other two sciences in the triumvirate.

At the present time the most important barriers to successful collaboration between the three sciences seem to be two. First, there is the ignorance of the content of other disciplines natural to those who have received intensive training in one discipline only. This can be overcome in large measure by collaboration between individuals trained in different disciplines. While the most effective collaboration is that which can be achieved by two disciplines under one skull, specialists can assist each other in the solution of joint problems if they can develop a common field of discourse. This brings us at once to the second difficulty, which is the lack of a consistent terminology shared by all three sciences. Even with the best intentions in the world, the specialist from one discipline often cannot understand what a specialist from another discipline is trying to say. The situation is complicated by the fact that many of the terms used in each of the three disciplines involved are still employed with a variety of meanings even within the disciplines themselves. In general, such terms possess a core of meaning accepted by all workers in the discipline surrounded by a shadowy zone of secondary meanings which lack such universal acceptance. Since a clear understanding of the terms and concepts employed by the various disciplines is vitally necessary for collaboration, a considerable part of this volume has been devoted to an attempt to define some of those which are in most frequent use. In this attempt I have tried to follow the democratic principle of majority rule, basing my definitions and explanations upon those meanings on which there seems to be general agreement and ignoring minority usages. It follows that such explanations will not make it possible for those trained in one discipline to understand everything that all workers in another discipline may be talking about. However, the attempt has been to provide a sort of lingua franca or trade language on the basis of which the simpler ideas and factual knowledge of the three disciplines can be exchanged. Whether I have succeeded in this only time can tell.

1

The Individual, Culture and Society

STUDIES of the individual, culture and society, and of their manifold interrelations are a response to the old admonition, "Man, know thyself." Most of the phenomena with which such studies deal have been tacitly recognized since time immemorial, but their investigation has been left largely to the philosopher and theologian. It is only within the last two or three generations that they have come to be considered an appropriate field for scientific research. Even now, such research is fraught with great difficulty. Although scientific attitudes are being invoked with increasing success, many of the recognized scientific techniques simply are not applicable to phenomena of these orders. Thus the very nature of the material precludes, in large part, the use of experimental methods. The intrinsic qualities of cultures and societies are such that it is impossible to produce them to order or to study them under rigid control conditions. The individual is more amenable to experimental techniques, but even he leaves much to be desired. Even as a small child he comes to the investigator with his own distinctive configuration of experience and of innate, biologically determined potentialities. These constitute an unsolved X in all equations; one which cannot be solved by any of the techniques now available to us. In theory, it might be possible to take care of the innate factors by developing, through controlled breeding, human strains of nearly uniform heredity. Given these, it might then be possible to observe the sorts of personality produced by various environmental conditions created by the investigator. However, such human guinea pigs belong to a future as remote as it is depressing in terms of all that we have been taught to value. Even the first step, that of developing pure strains, will have to await such an improbable event as the disappearance of incest taboos.

These limitations on the use of the experimental method are by no means the only difficulties which confront the investigator. Personalities, cultures and societies are all configurations in which the patterning and organization of the whole is more important than any of the component parts. Until very recent times the scientific trend has been toward the increasingly minute analysis of such configurations and the study of the parts rather than the whole. Even today, when the importance of configurations as such is generally recognized, there is a notable lack of techniques for dealing with them. Lastly, the lack of exact and demonstrable units for the measurement of most social and cultural phenomena is still a severe handicap. Until such units have been established, it will be impossible to apply many of the mathematical techniques which have proved so valuable in other fields of research.

The greatest technological advance within the general area under discussion has been made in connection with psychological studies. Here a long series of tests have been developed, many of which seem to give valid results. Most of these tests serve to reveal only certain aspects of personality content, not the personality configurations as a whole. On the basis of their results a series of individuals can be ranged with respect to a single quality, as intelligence, but such series will bear little relation to the order in which the same individuals can be ranged with respect to some other quality, as aggressiveness. The most recent and, from certain points of view most promising, advances in this field are the development of tests directed toward the personality configuration as a whole. These are still in their infancy, but such tests as the Rorschach and the Murray thematic aperception have already proved their value and promise well for the future.

Even when formal tests shall have been brought to the highest point of perfection they will not provide an answer to some of the most significant problems connected with the study of personality. Any test can throw light on the personality only as it exists at the time the test is given. Personalities are dynamic continuums, and although it is important to discover their content, organization and performance at a given point in time, it is still more important to discover the processes by which they develop, grow and change. With regard to these processes, formal tests can do no more than to give us a series of datum points along the individual's life trajectory. Very few records of this sort are now available. Until they become so, the best approach to the problems of personality development must remain the study and comparison of life histories as these can be obtained from the individuals themselves. Important work along this line has been done by the psychoanalysts, but even here much remains to be done in the development of objective techniques. In spite of the apparent validity of many of the psychoanalytic conclusions, most of these conclusions have been arrived at on the basis of subjective judgments and are not susceptible to the sort of proof required by workers in the exact sciences.

Many of the difficulties just enumerated will probably disappear with time. Pending the development of new techniques suited to the particular qualities of personality, culture, and society, investigators must arrive at their conclusions through the simple observation and comparison of their materials. Such an approach is comparable to that of the old-style naturalist rather than that of the modern student of animal behavior. However, it must not be forgotten that without the orientations provided by the naturalists' work many of the later developments would have been impossible. Students of human behavior, whether at the individual or the social level, have developed adequate descriptive techniques and a considerable understanding of the phenomena with which they have to deal. They have also developed an increasing awareness of the complexity of this material and of the close functional interdependence of the individual, society and culture. Following the earlier atomistic trends of scientific research, each of these has been treated as a separate field of investigation and made the subject of a distinct discipline. The individual has been assigned to Psychology, society to Sociology and culture

THE INDIVIDUAL, CULTURE AND SOCIETY 5

to Cultural Anthropology, although the last two sciences have shown a constant tendency to overlap in their investigations. It is now becoming apparent that the integration between the individual, society and culture is so close and their interaction so continuous that the investigator who tries to work with any one of them without reference to the other two soon comes to a dead end. There is still room for specialists and there are still vested interests which profit by keeping the various disciplines separate. However, it seems safe to say that the next few years will witness the emergence of a science of human behavior which will synthesize the findings of Psychology, Sociology and Anthropology. To this trinity Biology will probably be added in due course of time, but the relation between biological phenomena and psychological, social and cultural ones is still so poorly understood that it seems safest to omit it for the present.

In spite of the functional interrelations of the individual, society and culture, these three entities may, and indeed must, be differentiated for descriptive purposes. Although any particular individual is rarely of great importance to the survival and functioning of the society to which he belongs or the culture in which he participates, *the individual,* his needs and potentialities, lies at the foundation of all social and cultural phenomena. Societies are organized groups of individuals, and cultures are, in the last analysis, nothing more than the organized repetitive responses of a society's members. For this reason the individual is the logical starting point for any investigation of the larger configuration.

It may be assumed that it is the needs of the individual which provide the motivations for his behavior and which are, through this, responsible for the operation of society and culture. The needs of human beings appear to be more numerous and more varied than those of any other species. In addition to those which can be traced directly to physiological tensions, as the needs for food, for sleep, for escape from pain and for sexual satisfaction, man has a whole series of other needs whose connection with such tensions cannot be clearly demonstrated. These, for lack of a better term, we may call the *psychic needs*. Although the physiologically determined needs of the individual are usually called primary and the psychic ones secondary, such a distinction is justifiable mainly in terms of a genetic approach. The physiologically determined needs unquestionably appear first in the general course of evolution and are the first to manifest themselves in the individual life cycle. However, as motivations of adult behavior, physical and psychic needs seem to stand very much on a par. Perhaps in any long-continued conflict between the two the odds are on the physical needs, but the victory of the body's demands is never assured. Hunger strikers do persist to the end, and, as in Europe today, men die under torture rather than betray a friend or even give up an opinion. In the less violent exigencies of daily life we find the psychic needs again and again given precedence over the physical ones. Everyone knows the old proverb, "One must suffer to be beautiful."

In spite of the importance of psychic needs as motivations of behavior, we still know very little about them. Their genesis is obscure, and they have not even been adequately described or classified. Psychological states are tenuous things exceedingly difficult to deal with by exact objective methods. The nature and even the presence of psychic needs can only be deduced from the behavior to which they give rise. This behavior is so varied that it becomes largely a matter of choice whether it is to be referred to a small number of general motivations or a great number of specific ones. If the latter method is followed, the psychic needs can be expanded almost to infinity and most of the value inherent in taxonomic systems is thereby lost. A further difficulty in the development of an adequate classification of psychic needs arises from the fact that any human need, whether physical or psychic, rarely stands in a clear-cut one-to-one relationship with any pattern of overt behavior. When people act, especially if they do so in accordance with an established culture pattern, the action usually contributes toward satisfying several different needs simultaneously. Thus when we dress we do so partly to protect the body and partly to satisfy vanity or at least avoid censure. Under the circumstances it seems safest not to try to set up any classification of psychic needs, contenting ourselves with a brief discussion of a few of those which seem to be most general and most significant for the understanding of human behavior.

Perhaps the most outstanding and most continuously operative of man's psychic needs is that for emotional response from other individuals. The term emotional response is used advisedly, since the eliciting of mere behavioral responses may leave this need quite unsatisfied. Thus in a modern city it is quite possible for the individual to interact in formal, culturally established terms with a great number of other individuals and to obtain necessary services from them without eliciting any emotional responses. Under such circumstances his psychic need for response remains unsatisfied and he suffers from feelings of loneliness and isolation which are almost as acute as though no one else were present. In fact the experience tends to be more frustrating than genuine solitude. We all know what it means to be alone in a crowd. It is this need for response, and especially for favorable response, which provides the individual with his main stimulus to socially acceptable behavior. People abide by the mores of their societies quite as much because they desire approval as because they fear punishment.

This need for emotional response from others is so universal and so strong that many social scientists have regarded it as instinctive in the sense of being inborn. Whether it actually is so or whether it is a product of conditioning is a problem which may never be solved. The individual is so completely dependent upon others during infancy that he cannot survive without eliciting response from them. Such response would, therefore, come to be associated with the satisfaction of even his most elementary needs, and the desire for it might well survive even when he had developed techniques for satisfying them without assistance. On the other hand, there is good evidence that even young infants require a certain amount of emotional response for their well-being. Lack of it seems to be the only explanation for the high infant death-rate in even the best-run and most sanitary institutions, which far exceeds that under even unsanitary conditions of home life. As a leading psychoanalyst has succinctly phrased it in his lectures: "Babies who aren't loved don't live." [1] Since all individuals go through the experiences of infancy, the question of whether this need is innate or acquired is really an academic one. In either case its presence is universal.

A second and equally universal psychic need is that for security of the long-term sort. Thanks to the human ability to perceive time as a continuum extending beyond past and present into the future, present satisfactions are not enough as long as future ones remain uncertain. We are in constant need of reassurance, although the same time sense which makes it possible for us to worry about what may happen also makes it possible for us to postpone the satisfaction of present needs and put up with current discomforts in the expectation of future rewards. This need for security and for reassurance is reflected in innumerable forms of culturally patterned behavior. It leads the primitive craftsman to mingle magic with his technology and men at all levels of culture to imagine heavens in which the proper behavior of the present will be properly rewarded. In the light of our present very limited knowledge of psychological processes it seems idle to speculate as to the origins of this need. It is enough to recognize its importance as a motivation of forward-looking behavior.

The third and last psychic need which deserves mention at this time is that for novelty of experience.

[1] Dr. S. Ferenczi, quoted by Dr. Abram Kardiner.

This is probably less compulsive than the needs which have just been discussed; at least it rarely seems to come into play until most other needs have been satisfied. It finds its expression in the familiar phenomenon of boredom and leads to all sorts of experimental behavior. Just as in the case of the need for response, there is a possible explanation for it in terms of early conditioning. During early childhood the individual is constantly having new experiences, and, since many of these are pleasurable, the qualities of novelty and of pleasureableness may very well come to be linked in anticipation. On the other hand, the roots of this need may lie deeper. Even very small children show experimental tendencies, and Pavlov has recognized what he calls the exploratory reflex in animals.

The rôle of both physical and psychological needs in human behavior is strictly that of first causes. Without the spur which they provide, the individual would remain quiescent. He acts to relieve tensions, and this applies equally to overt actions and to such covert ones as learning and thinking. However, the forms which behavior assumes can never be explained in terms of the motivating needs alone. Such needs are forces whose expression is shaped by a multitude of other factors. The behavior which will suffice to satisfy any need or combination of needs must be organized with constant reference to the milieu in which the individual has to operate. This milieu includes factors of both environment and experience. Thus the behavior which will serve to meet the need for food is quite different in a modern city and in the wilderness. Moreover, the techniques which the individual will employ in each case will vary with his past experience. In the wilderness one who is accustomed to hunt will go about getting food in a quite different way from one who is not.

If the forms of human behavior cannot be explained in terms of the individual's needs, it is equally impossible to explain them in terms of his innate potentialities for action. These potentialities set ultimate limits to the forms which behavior can assume, but they leave an exceedingly wide range of possibilities. The choice of any one of these possibilities is determined by still other factors. The individual's behavior is immediately determined by his experience, and this, in turn, is derived from his contacts with his environment. It follows that an understanding of this environment is indispensable for the understanding both of individual personalities and of personality in general.

Although no two individuals, even identical twins reared in the same family, ever have identical environments, all human environments have certain features in common. We are prone to think of environment in terms of natural phenomena such as temperature, terrain or available food supply, factors which inevitably vary with the time and place. Although these things are reflected in the individual's experience and through this in his personality, they seem to be of rather minor importance in personality formation. Between the natural environment and the individual there is always interposed a human environment which is vastly more significant. This human environment consists of an organized group of other individuals, that is, a society, and of a particular way of life which is characteristic of this group, that is, a culture. It is the individual's interaction with these which is responsible for the formation of most of his behavior patterns, even his deep-seated emotional responses.

Unpleasant as the realization may be to egotists, very few individuals can be considered as more than incidents in the life histories of the societies to which they belong. Our species long ago reached the point where organized groups rather than their individual members became the functional units in its struggle for survival. Social living is as characteristic of *homo sapiens* as his mixed dentition or opposable thumb. However, in view of man's antecedents and nature, the most surprising thing about human societies is that they should have been developed at all. Our species is by no means the first to make the experiment of organized group living, but the gap which separates our societies from those of even our closest subhuman relatives is enormous. To find any real parallels to the human situation we must turn to the members of another phylum, the insects. These have developed societies only a shade less complicated than our own, but they have developed them by methods impossible to us. Insects have elaborated their instincts at the expense of their learning ability and, above all, at the expense of their inventiveness. Their whole evolutionary trend has been toward the production of elaborate, living automatons adjusted to fixed environments. They are beings in which a maximum of efficiency is combined with a minimum of individuality. Insects learn with difficulty and forget readily, but in most cases they can complete their brief life cycles without having to learn at all, still less to solve new problems. The adjustment of such automatons to functioning as members of an intricately organized society is only one step beyond their adjustment to functioning in a limited, stable natural environment and involves no new principle. Each ant or bee is fitted to his place in the community by a combination of structural specialization and instincts. He is organized both physically and psychologically to be a worker or soldier and cannot function in any other capacity. He has a minimum of individual needs and none which might bring him into conflict with other members of the same community. Unless singled out for a reproductive rôle, he (or she) has even been divested of those sexual drives which are such a fertile source of conflict among most vertebrates. In short, the social insects are less individuals than standardized, interchangeable units. From the time they are hatched they are so accurately fitted to their predestined social functions that they are incapable of departing from them. The class struggle could never develop in an anthill. Such units provide the perfect building blocks for a homogeneous, closely integrated and completely static social structure. The ant is born with everything that the most exacting dictator might wish his subjects to have.

In contrast to the social insects, man is the end product of an evolutionary process whose whole trend has been toward increasing individualization. Mammals have specialized in the ability to learn and, in

the higher stages of their development, to think. By the time our ancestors reached the human level they had lost most of their automatic responses, and those which did survive were of the simplest sort. Man has no instincts, at least in the sense in which we use that term when we talk about insect behavior. He has to learn or invent practically everything that he does. Thus every individual not only can but must develop his own patterns of behavior. Moreover, in spite of the partial fixation of such patterns through the process of habit formation, they never become set and unalterable in the way that instincts are. Coupled with the human ability to learn and to form habits there is an equally important ability to forget, to recognize new situations for what they are and to invent new behavior to meet them. The possibilities for individual variation in behavior are thus almost infinite. When several persons react in the same way to a particular situation, the cause must be sought in the experience which such individuals have in common. Obviously this fund of common experience will be much greater for the members of a single society than for members of different societies. However, there are certain sorts of experience which are common to all mankind. For example, every adult has been an infant dependent for his very survival on the care accorded him by other individuals. It is these common experiences and the common needs and abilities of mankind which are responsible for such uniformities of behavior as we can discern among mankind as a whole.

THE INDIVIDUAL, CULTURE AND SOCIETY

Intrinsically, the members of our species seem to have greater potentialities for differentiation and individualization than have the members of any other. The whole trend of our evolution has been away from the production of those standardized units which are the ideal building blocks for complex social structures. How we became socialized must remain a puzzle. Our subhuman relatives, who share our psychological qualities with differences of degree rather than of kind, are generally gregarious, but even anthropoid societies lack most of the specialization and differentiation of social functions which is so characteristic of our own. The gap between such societies and the simplest human ones is so wide that the development of our own patterns of social living must be regarded as an evolutionary tour de force. We are anthropoid apes trying to live like termites while lacking most of the termite equipment. One wonders whether we could not do it better with instincts.

Whatever the genesis of human societies may have been, all of them have certain features in common. The first and perhaps most important of these is that the society, rather than the individual, has become the significant unit in our species struggle for survival. Except by some unhappy accident, like that of Robinson Crusoe, all human beings live as members of organized groups and have their fate inextricably bound up with that of the group to which they belong. They cannot survive the hazards of infancy or satisfy their adult needs without the aid and coöperation of other individuals. Human life has passed long since from the stage of the individual workman to that of the assembly line in which each person makes his small, specific contribution to the finished product.

A second characteristic of societies is that they normally persist far beyond the life span of any one individual. Each of us is brought, by the accident of birth, into an organization which is already a going concern. Although new societies may come into being under certain conditions, most people are born, live and die as members of old ones. Their problem as individuals is not to assist in the organization of a new society but to adjust themselves to a pattern of group living which has long since crystallized. It may seem hardly necessary to point this out, but one finds in many writings a confusion between the genesis of social forms and the genesis of social behavior in the individual. How such an institution as the family originated is a problem of quite a different sort from that of how the individual becomes a functional, fully integrated member of a family.

Third, societies are functional, operative units. In spite of the fact that they are made up of individuals, they work as wholes. The interests of each of their component members are subordinated to those of the entire group. Societies do not even hesitate to eliminate some of these members when this is to the advantage of the society as a whole. Men go to war and are killed in war that the society may be protected or enriched, and the criminal is destroyed or segregated because he is a disturbing factor. Less obvious but more continuous are the daily sacrifices of inclinations and desires which social living requires of those who participate in it. Such sacrifices are rewarded in many ways, perhaps most of all by the favorable responses of others. Nevertheless, to belong to a society is to sacrifice some measure of individual liberty, no matter how slight the restraints which the society consciously imposes. The so-called free societies are not really free. They are merely those societies which encourage their members to express their individuality along a few minor and socially acceptable lines. At the same time they condition their members to abide by innumerable rules and regulations, doing this so subtly and completely that these members are largely unconscious that the rules exist. If a society has done its work of shaping the individual properly, he is no more conscious of most of the restrictions it has imposed than he is of the restraints which his habitual clothing imposes on his movements.

Fourth, in every society the activities necessary to the survival of the whole are divided and apportioned to the various members. There is no society so simple that it does not distinguish at least between men's and women's work, while most of them also set aside certain persons as intermediaries between man and the supernatural and as leaders to organize and direct the group's activities along certain lines. Such a division represents the absolute minimum, and in most societies we find it carried far beyond that point, with an assignment of various crafts to specialists and the appointment of social functionaries. This formal division of activities serves to give the society structure, organization and cohesion. It transforms the group of individuals who constitute the society from a mere amorphous mass into an organism. With each step in the differentiation of functions the individuals who perform these functions become increasingly dependent upon the whole. The merchant cannot exist without customers or the priest without a congregation.

It is the presence of such a system of organization which makes it possible for the society to persist through time. The mere biological processes of reproduction suffice to perpetuate the group, but not the society. Societies are like those historic structures, say our own frigate *Constitution,* which are replaced bit by bit while preserving the original pattern in its entirety. The simile is not quite satisfactory, since the structures of societies also change through time in response to the needs imposed by changing conditions. However, such changes are, for the most part, gradual, and patterning persists in spite of them. Societies perpetuate themselves as distinct entities by training the individuals who are born into the group to occupy particular places within the society's structure. In order to survive they must have not merely members but specialists, people who are able to do certain things superlatively well while leaving other things to other people. Seen from the standpoint of the individual, the process of socialization is thus one of learning what he should do for other people and what he is entitled to expect from them.

Both laboratory experiments and common sense tell us that the essence of successful learning lies in consistent reward or punishment. The behavior which always brings a desired result is learned much more quickly and readily than that which only brings it now and then. The successful training of the individual for a particular place in society depends upon the standardization of the behavior of the society's members. The boy who can learn to act like a man and to be a successful man when the time comes does so because everybody in his society agrees on how men should behave and rewards or punishes him in terms of how closely he adheres to or how far he departs from this standard. Such standards of behavior are called *culture patterns* by the anthropologist. Without them it would be impossible for any society either to function or to survive.

The concept of culture is so important that it will have to be dealt with in a separate chapter. For the present it is sufficient to define a culture as the way of life of any society. This way of life includes innumerable details of behavior but all of these have certain factors in common. They all represent the normal, anticipated response of any of the society's members to a particular situation. Thus, in spite of the infinite number of minor variations which can be found in the responses of various individuals, or even in those of the same individual at different times, it will be found that most of the people in a society will respond to a given situation in much the same way. In our own society, for example, nearly everybody eats three times a day and takes one of these meals approximately at noon. Moreover, individuals who do not follow this routine are regarded as queer. Such a consensus of behavior and opinion constitutes a culture pattern; the culture as a whole is a more or less organized aggregate of such patterns.

The culture as a whole provides the members of any society with an indispensable guide in all the affairs of life. It would be impossible either for them or for the society to function effectively without it. The fact that most members of the society will react to a given situation in a given way makes it possible for anyone to predict their behavior with a high degree of probability, even though never with absolute certainty. This predictability is a prerequisite for any sort of organized social living. If the individual is going to do things for others, he must have assurance that he will get a return. The presence of culture patterns, with their background of social approval and consequent potentialities for social pressure upon those who do not adhere to them, provides him with that assurance. Moreover, through long experience and largely by the use of the trial-and-error method, the culture patterns which are characteristic of any society have usually come to be closely adjusted to one another. The individual can get good results if he adheres to them, poor or even negative ones if he does not. The old proverb, "When in Rome do as the Romans do," is based on sound observation. In Rome or in any other society things are organized in terms of the local culture patterns and make few provisions for departure from them. The difficulties of an Englishman in quest of his tea in a small middle western town would be a case in point.

If the presence of culture patterns is necessary to the functioning of any society, it is equally necessary to its perpetuation. The structure, that is, system of organization, of a society is itself a matter of culture.

THE INDIVIDUAL, CULTURE AND SOCIETY 21

Although for purposes of description we can turn to spatial analogies and plot such a system in terms of positions, such positions cannot be defined adequately except in terms of the behavior expected of their occupants. Certain characteristics of age, sex or biological relationship may be prerequisites for the occupation of particular positions by the individual, but even the designation of such prerequisites is a cultural matter. Thus the positions of father and son in our own social system cannot be made clear by any statement of the biological relationship existing between the two. It is necessary to give an account of the culturally patterned behavior of the occupants of these positions toward each other. When it comes to such positions as those of employer and employee, we find it impossible to define them except in terms of what the occupants of these two positions are expected to do for (or possibly to) each other. A position in a social system, as distinct from the individual or individuals who may occupy it at a particular point in time, is actually a configuration of culture patterns. Similarly, the social system as a whole is a still more extensive configuration of culture patterns. This configuration provides the individual with techniques for group living and social interaction in much the same way that other pattern configurations, also within the total culture, provide him with techniques for exploiting the natural environment or protecting himself from supernatural dangers. Societies perpetuate themselves by teaching the individuals in each generation the culture patterns which belong with the positions in the society which they are expected to occupy. The new recruits to the society learn how to behave as husbands or chiefs or craftsmen and by so doing perpetuate these positions and with them the social system as a whole. Without culture there could be neither social systems of the human sort nor the possibility of adjusting new members of the group to them.

I realize that in the foregoing discussion of society and culture emphasis has been laid mainly upon the passive rôle of the individual and upon the way in which he is shaped by cultural and social factors. It is time now to present the other side of the picture. No matter how carefully the individual has been trained nor how successful his conditioning has been, he remains a distinct organism with his own needs and with capacities for independent thought, feeling and action. Moreover, he retains a considerable degree of individuality. His integration into society and culture goes no deeper than his learned responses, and although in the adult these include the greater part of what we call the personality, there is still a good deal of the individual left over. Even in the most closely integrated societies and cultures no two people are ever exactly alike.

Actually, the rôle of the individual with respect to society is a double one. Under ordinary circumstances, the more perfect his conditioning and consequent integration into the social structure, the more effective his contribution to the smooth functioning of the whole and the surer his rewards. However, societies have to exist and function in an ever changing world. The unparalleled ability of our species to adjust to changing conditions and to develop ever more effective responses to familiar ones rests upon the residue of individuality which survives in every one of us after society and culture have done their utmost. As a simple unit in the social organism, the individual perpetuates the status quo. As an individual he helps to change the status quo when the need arises. Since no environment is ever completely static, no society can survive without the occasional inventor and his ability to find solutions for new problems. Although he frequently invents in response to pressures which he shares with other members of his society, it is his own needs which spur him on to invention. The first man who wrapped a skin about him or fed a fire did this not because he was conscious that his society needed these innovations but because he felt cold. To pass to a higher level of culture complexity, no matter how injurious an existing institution may be to a society in the face of changing conditions, the stimulus to change or abandon it never comes from the individual upon whom it entails no hardship. New social inventions are made by those who suffer from the current conditions, not by those who profit from them.

An understanding of the double rôle of individuals as individuals and as units in society will provide a key to many of the problems which trouble students of human behavior. In order to function successfully as a unit in society, the individual must assume certain stereotyped forms of behavior, that is, culture patterns. A great many of these culture patterns are oriented toward the maintenance of society rather than the satisfaction of individual needs. Societies are organisms of a sort, and it has become common practice to speak of their having needs of their own as distinct from those of the individuals who compose them. Such usage carries unfortunate implications, since the qualities of societies are quite different from those of living organisms. It is safer to express the necessities implicit in the social situation by saying that a society can neither endure through time nor function successfully at any point in time unless the associated culture fulfills certain conditions. It must include techniques for indoctrinating new individuals in the society's system of values and for training them to occupy particular places in its structure. It must also include techniques for rewarding socially desirable behavior and discouraging that which is socially undesirable. Lastly, the behavior patterns which compose the culture must be adjusted to one another in such a way as to avoid conflict and prevent the results of one pattern of behavior from negating those of another. All societies have developed cultures which fulfill these conditions, although the processes involved in their development are still obscure.

The culture patterns upon which any society depends for its survival must be established as patterns of habitual response on the part of its members. This is rendered possible by man's extraordinary ability to absorb teaching. Teaching is used advisedly since something more than mere learning from accidental and unorganized experience is involved. All human beings receive deliberate and purposeful instruction from their elders. Complex patterns of behavior are transferred from generation to generation in this way. The individual's incentive for assuming these patterns lies in the satisfaction which they afford to his personal needs, especially his need for favorable response from others. However, from the point of view of his society such satisfactions are important mainly as bait. He learns the patterns as wholes, and these wholes subtend the necessities of social living quite as much as they subtend his own needs. He takes the bait of immediate personal satisfaction and is caught upon the hook of socialization. He would learn to eat in response to his own hunger drive, but his elders teach him to "eat like a gentleman." Thus, in later years, his hunger drive elicits a response which will not only satisfy it but do so in a way acceptable to his society and compatible with its other culture patterns. Through instruction and imitation the individual develops habits which cause him to perform his social rôle not only effectively but largely unconsciously. This ability to integrate into a single configuration elements of behavior some of which serve to meet individual needs, others to satisfy social necessities, and to learn and transmit such configurations as wholes is the thing that makes human societies possible. By assuming such configurations and establishing them as habits the individual is adjusted to occupy a particular position in society and to perform the rôle associated with that position.

The fact that most human behavior is taught in the form of organized configurations rather than simply developed by the individual on the basis of experience, is of the utmost importance to personality studies. It means that the way in which a person responds to a particular situation often provides a better clue to what his teaching has been than to what his personality is. In general, all the individuals who occupy a given position in the structure of a particular society will respond to many situations in very much the same way. That any one individual of such a group manifests this response proves nothing about his personality except that he has normal learning ability. His personal predispositions will be revealed not by his culturally patterned responses but by his deviations from the culture pattern. It is not the main theme of his behavior but the overtones which are significant for understanding him as an individual. In this fact lies the great importance of cultural studies for personality psychology. Until the psychologist knows what the norms of behavior imposed by a particular society are and can discount them as indicators of personality he will be unable to penetrate behind the façade of social conformity and cultural uniformity to reach the authentic individual.

2

The Concept of Culture

THE realization that different societies have different ways of life goes back to hoary antiquity. The first man who wandered into a strange camp and found that he could not talk to the people there nor understand everything that he saw, must have had the fact of cultural difference brought home to him. Also, if he was lucky enough to get back to his own camp alive, his observations must have provided him with material for numerous fireside talks. Most people are interested in the curious behavior of other people and like to hear about it. The meat of any really good traveler's tale is not the strange places that it tells about but the queer people. Stories of alien customs are the gossip of our species and are listened to with the same mixture of smug self-satisfaction and unacknowledged envy which makes the smaller gossip of one's own society so delectable. The greatest of all international gossips, Herodotus, devotes much of his history to what we would call today descriptions of culture. He even goes so far as to point out some of the more outstanding differences between Greek and Egyptian customs, with genuine surprise that these barbarians retired into the house to perform their excretory functions instead of taking to the street in civilized Greek fashion.

Such bits of information have been recorded by all sorts of writers, ancient and modern, and have provided a steadily accumulating mass of data which the modern student of society and culture still finds of use. However, until very recent times, facts of this sort have been collected in a spirit much the same as that of the amateur collector of Indian relics. The customs of non-European groups were treated as curios with which to astonish the uninformed, and the rarer and more bizarre they were the greater the pride of the discoverer. Writers of this period always took the customs of their own society for granted, and even fifty years ago the description of a modern European culture pattern, unless it was that of some isolated peasant community, would have been considered as much out of place in an ethnographic treatise as a kitchen knife in a cabinet full of arrowheads. Similar periods of curio-hunting can be found at the beginning of most sciences and seem to be a necessary stage in their development. They turn the common human tendency to accumulate novelties to the useful purpose of gathering and preserving material which later workers can study and organize. In going over these early ethnographies the modern student is often irritated by the blandly unconscious omissions of their authors, but he must satisfy himself with the old adage that half a loaf is better than no bread.

The change from curio-collecting to scientific research in human behavior was ushered in by certain important modifications in the workers' point of view.

The first and perhaps most significant of these was the realization that, for the understanding of human life in general, the similarities between the customs of various societies were more important than the differences. Thus the fact that all societies have some sort of family organization is much more significant in the long run than the fact that Thibetan women of the lower class usually have several husbands. The first provides a clue to the needs and potentialities of mankind in general, while the second constitutes a small, specific problem which can be solved only in terms of local conditions and local history. Even when such a problem has been solved, the answer will not help us much in predicting how the members of other societies will behave.

The second change in viewpoint, which appeared somewhat later than the first, was the realization that there are many problems which can be solved only by studying the way of life of particular societies as wholes. Although we can learn certain things about human behavior by comparing the forms which a particular institution, say marriage, assumes in various societies, there are many other things which we can learn only by seeing how marriage operates in particular societies and the relation which it bears to the other institutions present. This approach is still more imperative when we try to understand the behavior of individuals. Although these may react to particular situations in particular ways, their personalities are shaped by their experience with their society's way of life as a whole. With the development of personality studies the concept of culture has thus become of primary importance to the psychologist as well as the sociologist and anthropologist. It can be one of the most useful tools in the psychologist's research equipment, but its implications and limitations must be clearly understood as a preliminary to its effective use.

The term *culture,* as it is employed in scientific studies, carries none of the overtones of evaluation which attach to it in popular usage. It refers to the total way of life of any society, not simply to those parts of this way which the society regards as higher or more desirable. Thus culture, when applied to our own way of life, has nothing to do with playing the piano or reading Browning. For the social scientist such activities are simply elements within the totality of our culture. This totality also includes such mundane activities as washing dishes or driving an automobile, and for the purposes of cultural studies these stand quite on a par with "the finer things of life." It follows that for the social scientist there are no uncultured societies or even individuals. Every society has a culture, no matter how simple this culture may be, and every human being is cultured, in the sense of participating in some culture or other.

Actually, the work of the social scientist must begin with the investigation of *cultures,* the ways of life which are characteristic of particular societies. *Culture,* as he uses the term, represents a generalization based upon the observation and comparison of a series of *cultures.* It bears much the same relation to these individual cultures that "the spider monkey" of a naturalist's description bears to the innumerable individual spider monkeys who together constitute the species. When the anthropologist says that culture has such and such characteristics, what he really means is that all cultures have these characteristics in common. It is the cultures, each linked to a particular society, which are the organized, functional entities, and it is against the background of a specific culture, not of culture in general, that the individual must be studied.

Although the term *a culture* has been used for many years to designate the way of life of a particular society, its exact meaning in terms of content is still vague at certain points. Like a number of other concepts employed in the social sciences, that of *a culture* has been undergoing a process of gradual delimitation through usage. Such a process accords well with the needs of new and rapidly developing sciences and is the only really workable one in the absence of any ultimate authority to which differences of opinion can be referred. When a new term appears, workers in the particular science tend to employ it with much the same meanings but with individual differences in the exact connotations which they give it. In time the common elements of meaning achieve general recognition, and the individual ones are discarded. The end of this process is the emergence of a clear-cut concept designated by a single term whose meaning is clear to all workers in the particular field. However, even when such agreement has been reached, the term employed may be susceptible of several different definitions. It is the essence of any definition that it selects certain aspects of the total concept for which the term stands and stresses these at the expense of other aspects. This emphasis, and the consequent value of the definition for a particular purpose, will depend upon the particular end which the definer has in view. There are many possible definitions of *a culture,* each of which is useful in connection with investigations of a particular sort. Thus it could be quite correctly defined as "the social heredity of a society's members," but this would be of little help to students of personality formation.

On the basis of common usage and understanding and with regard to the special interests of students of personality, I will venture the following definition: "A culture is the configuration of learned behavior and results of behavior whose component elements are shared and transmitted by the members of a particular society." Like all definitions, this requires some amplification and explanation. The term *configuration* implies that the various behaviors and results of behavior which compose a culture are organized into a patterned whole. This feature of culture involves a number of problems which need not be dealt with here. *Learned behavior* limits the activities which are to be classed as part of any given culture configuration to those whose forms have been modified by the learning process. This limitation has the sanction of long usage. Neither instinctive behavior nor the basic needs or tensions which provide the ultimate motivations for behavior in the individual have ever been regarded as parts of culture in spite of their obvious influence upon culture. The elimination of these phenomena from the culture concept still leaves it an exceedingly wide scope. As has been noted in the previous chapter, man appears to have very few unconditioned reflexes

THE CONCEPT OF CULTURE

aside from those connected with his physiological processes. Although his behavior is motivated by his needs, the forms which it assumes are normally conditioned by experience. Thus although eating is a response to the individual's need for nourishment, the way in which he eats depends upon how he has learned to eat. The term *behavior* in the phrase under discussion is to be taken in the broadest sense to include all the activities of the individual, whether overt or covert, physical or psychological. Thus for the purposes of this definition, learning, thinking, and so on are to be considered quite as much forms of behavior as are the coördinated muscular movements involved in technological processes.

The term *results of behavior* refers to phenomena of two quite different orders, psychological and material. The former include those results of behavior which are represented in the individual by psychological states. Thus attitudes, value systems and knowledge would all be included under this head. To class these phenomena as results of behavior may appear a tour de force, but they are unquestionably established in the individual as a result of his interaction with his environment and consequent learning. At the same time, they cannot be classed as learned *behavior*, since they lack the dynamic qualities implied by this term. Like the realities of the external environment, they exercise a directive influence on the development of behavior patterns. Thus when confronted by a new situation the individual will react to it not only in terms of its objective reality but also in terms of the attitudes, values and knowledge which he has acquired as a result of his past experience. The native who meets a white man for the first time may worship him as a god, treat him as an honored guest or attack him on sight, his line of action depending entirely on factors of the sort under discussion.

The inclusion of material results of behavior in the phenomena covered by the culture concept may meet with objections from certain sociologists, but it is sanctioned by anthropological usage as old as the term *culture* itself. The objects habitually made and used by the members of any society have always been known collectively as its "material culture" and regarded as an integral part of the culture configuration. The real problem in this case is whether the objects themselves are to be regarded as a part of culture or whether the content of the culture configuration should be limited to the psychological elements to which the objects correspond. In other words, shall we include the axe or simply the ideas shared by the members of a society as to how an axe should look and what its qualities should be? The inclusion of material objects complicates the work of investigators who try to use the culture concept for certain purposes, but for students of personality the elimination of material culture would constitute a loss rather than a gain. The environment in which any individual develops and functions always includes a great variety of man-made objects, and the effect of contact with these on the developing personality may be considerable. Thus this aspect of the total environment may operate either to stimulate or to inhibit the development of manual dexterity or even the development of more basic features of the

THE CONCEPT OF CULTURE

personality, such as generalized attitudes of timidity or self-reliance. The early experience of a child reared among gadgets or in a house full of fragile bric-a-brac will be quite different from that of one reared in a dwelling where there is nothing he can injure or which can injure him. Even our own custom of sitting and lying on raised furniture involves a series of infantile hazards quite lacking in a society whose members habitually sit and lie on the floor.

The phrase *shared and transmitted* limits the content of culture configurations still further. In the present case *shared* must be taken to mean that a particular pattern of behavior, attitude or piece of knowledge is common to two or more of a society's members. It carries no implications of coöperative activity or joint ownership. Any item of behavior, and so on, which is peculiar to a single individual in a society is not to be considered as a part of the society's culture. However, such individual peculiarities may, in due course of time, become a part of the culture. Actually, all cultural innovations originate either with some one person or with a very small group of persons. Thus a new technique for weaving baskets would not be classed as a part of culture as long as it was known only to one person. It would be classed as a part of culture as soon as it came to be shared by other individuals.

To further clarify the limitations imposed on culture content by this factor of sharing, it is necessary to remember that cultures are continuums. The sharing which justifies the inclusion of a particular item in the culture configuration must be determined with relation to the social-cultural continuum, not with relation to a culture as it exists at a particular point in time. Thus the fact that there is only one practicing physician in a particular community in 1943 does not mean that the skills of the physician are not to be regarded as a part of the community's culture. The community will normally have included other physicians with similar skills in the past and will include still others in the future. There is thus a sharing of particular types of knowledge and behavior through time, even if it is lacking at a particular point in time. This immediately raises the question of whether items of individual knowledge or behavior which later achieve cultural status are to be rated as parts of culture from their inception. On logical grounds they probably should be, but since their position can be established only in retrospect, and since at the time of their inception they do not function as elements in the operative culture configuration of the society, the problem is largely an academic one.

One further qualification with respect to the term *shared* is necessary. It must not be taken to imply that elements which are to be regarded as part of a culture configuration have to be shared by all members of a society either through time or at any particular point in time. Actually, it would be impossible to find any element of culture which had been shared by all members of a society throughout that society's entire duration. Cultures change and grow, discarding certain elements and acquiring new ones in the course of their history. As a result of this process, they may experience an almost complete turnover in content and profound changes in pattern if the associated society endures

THE CONCEPT OF CULTURE

long enough and is subject to enough vicissitudes. Thus there are many places in the world where, on the basis of physical anthropological evidence, the modern population is a direct descendant of the Neolithic one and where the cultural and social continuity has never been interrupted; yet the life of these moderns has few features in common with that of their Neolithic forebears. Even if we take any social-cultural configuration at a particular point in time, we will find that there are no elements of the culture which are shared by all members of the society. Although some of them may be shared by all adults, even these are not shared by small children, while many adult ideas and activities are shared only by the members of certain groupings within the society, as men, women or specialized craftsmen. Such specialties must none the less be regarded as integral parts of the culture configuration. They are adjusted to other elements within the configuration and contribute to the well-being of the society as a whole.

The term *transmitted* requires little discussion. The sharing of elements of behavior, and so on, is dependent upon their transmission from one individual to another through instruction or imitation. These processes operate through time, and most of the elements which compose culture configurations are transmitted from generation to generation and endure far beyond the life span of any one member of the society. From the point of view of the individual, the culture of the society in which he is reared constitutes his social, as distinct from his biological, heredity. It provides him with a series of adaptations to the environment in which he must live and function. These adaptations, embodied in patterns of behavior, have been developed by earlier members of his society as a result of their experiences and are passed on to him by way of his learning processes. They save him from the necessity of going through many frequently painful experiences in order to make successful adjustments. The transfer of such behavioral adaptations parallels in many respects the transfer of the structural and physiological adaptations developed by the individual's ancestors as a result of mutation and selection. Thus in a West African Negro society the cultural techniques for getting food in the jungle, developed by past generations, will be transmitted to the individual through learning. A high degree of immunity to malaria, also developed by past generations, will be transmitted to him by heredity. Both will be necessary for survival under the local conditions.

It can be seen from the foregoing discussion of culture that the concept includes phenomena of at least three different orders: material, that is, products of industry; kinetic, that is, overt behavior (since this necessarily involves movement); and psychological, that is, the knowledge, attitudes and values shared by the members of a society. For our present purposes the phenomena of the first two orders may be classed together as constituting the *overt* aspect of a culture. Those of the third order, that is, psychological phenomena, constitute the *covert* aspect of a culture. Both these aspects are equally real and equally important for the understanding of human behavior, but they present different problems for the investigator. The overt aspect of any culture is concrete and tangible. It is subject to direct observation and record, and there is no conclusion with regard to it which cannot be checked with the aid of such mechanical appliances as the motion-picture camera and phonograph. Any errors which may arise with respect to it will be due to nothing more than faulty observation and can easily be corrected.

The recording of covert culture presents problems of a quite different sort. This aspect of culture is a matter of psychological states, and the nature and even the existence of such states can only be inferred from the overt behavior to which they give rise. The problem of establishing the covert patterns within a culture is much the same as that of ascertaining the content and organization of an individual's personality, and investigations are subject to the same sources of error. Although we are witnessing a steady improvement in techniques for the objective study of psychological phenomena, there is still a very large element of subjective judgment involved even in the diagnosis of individual personalities. When we attempt such a diagnosis for the members of a whole society, or even for those of a particular group within a society, the possibilities of error are greatly increased.

Anthropological field workers are rarely trained in the use of the more elaborate and exact techniques of psychological testing, and even when they are it is rarely possible for them to apply such tests to more than a small sample of the society. It is almost impossible to make this a true random sample. The individuals with whom the field worker is brought into contact are not mere units in a statistical table but actual people whose reactions to the investigator will be as varied as those of persons in our own society. Since they are usually quite unable to understand the purpose of the tests, there is an even stronger resistance to taking them than one encounters in our own society. As a result, the only subjects usually available for testing are (*a*) those who are congenial with the observer and submit through friendship and (*b*) those who are at such an economic level that their resistance can be overcome by the small fees usually available for such work. There is thus a very real, if unconscious, selection of subjects which introduces a margin of error when one attempts to refer the test results to the society as a whole.

When it comes to those continuous contacts and close acquaintances which are necessary for informal judgments of personality, the selective factor becomes even more important. The observer living in an alien society can establish close and friendly relationships with only a small number of individuals. Who these individuals will be will vary with the personalities and interests of both parties. The only natives whom an investigator will come to know really well will be those whom he finds congenial and who find him so. Conclusions based upon such a selected sample may be far from applicable to the group as a whole. Thus in my own experience of several different "primitive" groups I have always found a considerable number of individuals who were genuinely sceptical with regard to the supernatural, but it would be quite wrong to regard such attitudes as general or even common in the societies in question. The only check on such potential sources of error which is possible at the present time is to have each society studied by several investigators. These investigators should work independently and should be as diverse in their own personality configurations as possible.

The difficulties just cited do not mean that it is impossible to obtain a clear picture of the covert culture of any society. They only mean that it is difficult and that the conclusions set forth by a single observer are not to be taken as necessarily the last word on the subject. Students of personality who attempt to use ethnological reports should realize, however, that the statement that the members of a particular society are cowardly, or avaricious, or indifferent to children involves elements of selected acquaintance and subjective judgment which are quite lacking in such statements as that they keep their children on cradle boards or make wooden bowls or hold dances at the time of the full moon.

There is one other point in connection with the distinction between overt and covert culture which is of some significance for students of personality. It is the overt aspect of culture which is the principal agent in culture transmission. The psychological states which constitute covert culture are not, in themselves, transferable. Other individuals, whether alien observers or young members of the same society, can be made conscious of the existence of such states only through the overt behaviors in which they find expression. It is the contact with, and experience derived from, the overt culture of his society which re-creates in each individual the shared psychological states which constitute the covert culture. Thus he comes to share in his society's culture pattern of fearing some harmless object, say a human skull, because other members of the society manifest fear of it in his presence or tell him that it is to be feared. Similarly, he assumes his society's culture pattern of attaching high values to certain goals because he sees other members of the society striving to attain these goals.

It is hoped that the foregoing will have made clear what the anthropologist means by culture and the various orders of phenomena which are included within the concept. In their attempts to use this concept as a tool for research even the anthropologists sometimes become confused. Thus they frequently fail to distinguish even in their descriptive studies between cultures as they exist through time and cultures as they exist at a particular point in time, although these two aspects of the concept present different problems and call for somewhat different methods of approach. This distinction is more important for students of cultural processes than for psychologists. The latter need only concern themselves with the brief segment of a culture continuum which corresponds with the life spans of the individuals whom they are investigating. However, the failure of many anthropological writers to distinguish clearly between the current conditions in the cultures which they describe and those which survive only in the memory of old informants may create difficulties for the psychologists who try to use such accounts. Thus a description of a tribal culture which mingles past and present culture patterns indiscriminately cannot be used effectively as a background for studying the personalities of the tribe members.

Of much greater importance to the psychologist is the anthropologist's almost constant failure to distinguish clearly between the reality of a culture as a configuration of behaviors, and so on, and the construct which he develops on the basis of this reality and uses as a tool for the description and manipulation of cultural data. The lack of a terminology which will serve to distinguish clearly between these two aspects of the culture concept has been a source of endless trouble not only to psychologists and anthropologists but also to those logicians and philosophers who have attempted to deal with the culture concept. As an aid to clarification I have ventured to coin the terms *real culture* and *culture construct* and will try to make plain the meaning of each.

The real culture of any society consists of the actual behavior, and so on, of its members. It includes a vast number of elements, no two of which are identical. No two persons ever react to a given stimulus in exactly the same way, and even the same person will react to such a stimulus differently at different times. Every individual bit of behavior differs in some particular from every other bit. To increase the complexity, no two stimuli are ever identical, either. However, the individual is able to develop successful and more or less automatic adjustments to his environment in spite of this intrinsic variability. He generalizes with respect to stimuli of a particular sort, lumping them together on the basis of their similarities and ignoring their differences. Thus a student learns that the ringing of a bell in the classroom means that the hour is up and ignores the minor day-to-day differences in the tone and duration of the signal. Similarly, his response to such a signal, although never twice exactly the same, will be much the same on all occasions. Passing from the individual to groups of individuals having a common background of knowledge and experience, we find a very similar situation. To revert to the classroom, all the experienced students will prepare to leave the room when they hear the bell ring. Although their individual preparations will differ in detail, the differences will normally fall within a rather narrow range of variation. Thus the students are fairly certain to close their notebooks and gather up whatever objects they have brought to class with them but exceedingly unlikely to take off their overcoats or rubbers.

It follows that the innumerable items of behavior which constitute a real culture can be sorted out on the basis of the situations which normally evoke them. Each generalized situation will be linked with a particular series of behaviors all of which have numerous features in common. Moreover, the variations in such a series will ordinarily be found to fall within certain easily recognizable limits. These limits may be set by purely practical considerations. Thus there are only a few ways in which coiled baskets can be made. They may also be established by social sanctions. Thus every society has certain recognized techniques for getting married or for approaching a superior to ask a favor. In either case, behaviors which fall outside the normal range simply do not bring the desired results. This fact will be tacitly recognized by the members of the society themselves. Behaviors which fall within the effective range will be considered normal, while those which fall outside it will be regarded as queer and, frequently, as reprehensible.

Such a range of normal responses to a particular situation may be designated as a pattern within the real culture. Conversely, the real culture may be conceived of as a configuration composed of a great number of such patterns all of which are, in greater or less degree, mutually adjusted and functionally interrelated. The important thing to remember is that each of the *real culture patterns* is not a single item of behavior but a series of behaviors varying within certain limits.

The variability of the behaviors included in any real culture presents a serious problem even at the level of pure description. It is obviously impossible to describe all the items of behavior which together constitute the culture. Even the series of behaviors which constitute the normal responses to each of the situations to which a society's members may react cannot be given in full. In order to present a comprehensible picture of any culture, or to manipulate cultural data, the investigator has to develop a *culture construct*. He establishes the mode of the finite series of variations which are included within each of the real culture patterns and then uses this mode as a symbol for the real culture pattern. Thus if the investigator finds that the members of a particular society are in the habit of going to bed sometime between eight and ten o'clock but that the mode for his series of cases falls at quarter-past nine, he will say that going to bed at quarter-past nine is one of the patterns of their culture. Such a modal derivative may be termed a *culture construct pattern*. The total culture construct is developed by combining all the culture construct patterns which have been developed in this way. It bears very much the same relation to the real culture that the construct patterns bear to the real patterns. Although the culture construct may not be in exact correspondence with the real culture at any point, it provides a brief and convenient approximation of the conditions existing within the real culture. Experience has shown that on the basis of such constructs it is possible not only to study the structure of real cultures and the interrelations of their component patterns but also to predict the behavior of a society's members in various situations with a high degree of probability. Culture constructs are nothing more than tools to be used by the investigator, but they are indispensable tools. Their development is justified by their subsequent utility.

To sum up, a *real culture* consists of the sum total of the behaviors of a society's members in so far as these behaviors are learned and shared. A *real culture pattern* represents a limited range of behaviors within which the responses of a society's members to a particular situation will normally fall. Thus various individuals can behave differently while still behaving in accordance with the real culture pattern. A *culture construct pattern* corresponds to the mode of the variations within a real culture pattern. Once these distinctions are clearly understood, it is easy to resolve most of the difficulties involved in relating individual experience and behavior to cultural data presented in construct form.

The value of culture construct patterns for summarizing most of the environmental influences significant in personality formation becomes obvious when we consider the conditions which surround the developing individual in all societies. All human beings normally develop and function as members of organized groups sharing a common habitat. It follows that most of the environment with which the individual interacts consists of other individuals or of man-made objects. This is especially true during the early phases of the life cycle when the foundations for personality development are being laid. Adult care interposes a screen between the small child and most of the natural environment of his society. The Eskimo infant, snug inside his mother's parka, is little affected by arctic temperatures. Most of the individual's early experience derives from the behavior of other persons. This behavior may be directed toward him, as in the case of adult techniques for child care or adult responses to childish behavior. It may also be directed toward ends which the child himself desires, thus leading him to observe and imitate it. In either case the behavior of others provides the child with experience on the basis of which he develops his own behavior patterns. Thus in our own society the disapproval which adults manifest when a child eats with his fingers will soon lead him to give up the habit, while his observation of how some adult goes about getting the jam or opening the cookie jar, will provide him with a pattern of behavior which he can later, and perhaps privately, put into effect.

Most of the events which have enduring consequences in personality formation are of a repetitive sort. Although some unusual and violent episode may have traumatic results, the essence of personality development, as of the more direct and immediate forms of learning, is the repetition of particular stimuli and of the behaviors which provide adequate responses to them. Under the normal conditions of social living, most of the external stimuli to which the child responds originate in the behavior of other individuals. Although this behavior will never be identical on any two occasions, its variations will nearly always fall within one or another of those limited series of behaviors which, as has been said, constitute the patterns within real culture. Moreover, there seems to be a fairly close correlation between the mode of the varying behaviors within such a series and the type of experience which the individual derives from his contacts with persons operating within the series, that is, real culture pattern. In other words, the varying behaviors within a particular culture pattern function, with respect to their effects on the individual, as what the physicists call *convergent phenomena*. Their differences tend to cancel out in the long run, so that their cumulative result in personality formation is very much the same as that which would be produced by repetitions of a single item of behavior standing at the mode of the series constituting the pattern. Thus the experience derived from eating lunch some-

THE CONCEPT OF CULTURE 49

time between twelve and one but most frequently at about half-past twelve will be very much the same as that derived from always eating lunch at half-past twelve.

One must hasten to add that this does not imply that the results of contact with a particular pattern of real culture will be the same for all individuals. We have abundant evidence that such is not the case. The experience which any individual derives from participating in any situation is influenced not only by the situation per se but also by his own potentialities and perceptions. Thus a culture pattern by which a boy is required to keep the wood box filled will produce one sort of experience in a strong, active child, another sort in a feeble, sickly one. A gypsy at the door will mean one thing to a child who has been told that all gypsies are kidnappers, something quite different to one who is ignorant of this bit of folklore. Even in cases where the external situation can be treated as a constant, these individual factors will cause it to produce different results in different persons.

Since a culture construct is the sum total of the modes of the various patterns which compose a real culture and since the mode of each pattern is closely correlated with the type of experience which individuals derive from their contacts with it, it follows that a culture construct can be used to summarize the social-cultural environment from which the members of any society derive the bulk of their experience. Although all the members of any society may not have first-hand experience of all the patterns within its culture, all of them will be brought into contact with many of the same patterns. These patterns, as represented in the culture construct, can be treated as constants in studies of personality formation. They provide a uniform background against which the varying responses and personality configurations of a society's members can be studied and compared. The establishment of such a stable frame of reference is an indispensable aid to personality studies.

The relation of culture patterns to the experience common to the members of a particular society can be made clearer by a specific example. Let us suppose that it is the pattern in a society to feed infants whenever they cry and not to feed them unless they cry. Given the variations within such a culture pattern which must result from the exigencies of everyday life, we can be sure that not all members of this society were fed whenever they cried. However, all of them will have been fed on most of the occasions when they cried and not fed when they did not cry. As a result, all of them will have had abundant opportunity to develop crying as a first response leading to the satisfaction of their hunger needs. Their experience, in spite of all the variable factors involved in the operation of the culture pattern and in their individual differences, will have much in common. All members of the particular society will resemble one another in this respect much more closely than they will resemble the members of some other society in which it is the culture pattern to feed children on strict schedule and in which crying is either ignored or punished.

The utility of culture constructs for personality study is not limited to summarizing the social-cultural environment common to the members of a society. The patterns within such a construct are also of great assistance in the diagnosis of individual personalities. Each construct pattern represents the mode of the varying behaviors of a series of individuals with respect to a particular situation. It will be found that although the varying behaviors of any one individual with respect to this situation normally will all fall within the range of the real culture pattern, they will rarely if ever show the whole of this range. They will correspond to a particular segment of it, and the individual mode within this segment may differ considerably from that for the culture pattern as a whole. The difference between this individual mode and the culture construct pattern will reflect the compromise which every individual has to make between the culture patterns of his society and his own inclinations. Such individual deviations may not be of great significance for personality diagnosis as long as they are present in the case of only a few culture patterns. Thus if the pattern requires a man to make large and frequent gifts to his father-in-law and he actually gives as little as possible, it may mean no more than that he dislikes his father-in-law or hopes to terminate his marriage. However, if the modes of an individual's behavior ranges show a consistent displacement with respect to a large series of culture construct patterns, it is safe to assume that the direction of this displacement reflects some particular quality of the individual. Thus if the man just mentioned shirks his responsibilities not only to his father-in-law but in most other situations requiring expenditure, it is a fairly sure indication that he is stingy. Actually, we all make constant if unconscious use of this factor of deviation from the culture pattern mode in our day-to-day judgments of the personalities of other individuals. We do not phrase the norms of behavior in culture pattern terms, but we know what they are and are quick to recognize deviations and to class other people accordingly.

Before closing this discussion of culture it may be well to mention one other feature of the culture pattern situation. In addition to real culture patterns and the culture construct patterns developed on the basis of the investigator's observation and plotting of behavior, all cultures include a certain number of what may be called *ideal patterns*. These are abstractions which have been developed by the members of a society themselves. They represent the consensus of opinion on the part of the society's members as to how people should behave in particular situations. The extent to which such ideal patterns have been developed will vary greatly in different societies. Some groups are much more conscious of the existence of culture and much more prone to generalize about behavior than others. However, no group ever develops ideal patterns of behavior corresponding to all situations. Even in the most analytically minded and culture-conscious societies the investigator finds again and again that informants are quite unable to tell what the proper behavior in a particular situation would be and have to fall back on relating what happened on various occasions when this situation arose. This lack of ideal patterns is the more striking since comparison of the narratives usually reveals the presence of a real culture pattern with a recognizable mode of variation. In general, ideal patterns appear to be developed most frequently with respect to those situations which a society regards as of primary importance and particularly with respect to those involving the interaction of individuals in different positions in the social system.

Ideal patterns may not and indeed usually do not agree with the construct patterns which the investigator develops through his observations of actual behavior. In some cases this lack of agreement may reflect nothing more than a failure of the ideal pattern to keep abreast of the realities of a changing culture. It is based on memories of things as they were rather than on observation of things as they are. In other cases the ideal pattern probably never has been in agreement with the mode of the real culture pattern. It represents a desideratum, a value which has always been more honored in the breach than in the observance. In either case ideal patterns exercise some normative effect, discouraging too wide divergence from the standards which they set. However, when such ideal patterns become thoroughly verbalized and crystallized they tend to lose some measure of their influence. They acquire an independent existence and instead of representing the proper response to a particular situation become themselves the proper response to a particular question. Our own ideal pattern, "Little children love one another," survives as such a verbal response in the face of both personal memories and daily observations to the contrary. Such verbalizations are themselves patterns in real culture, but they are to be classed with the literature of a society and give no more indication of the actual behavior of its members than do any other bits of folklore. It is exceedingly desirable, therefore, for those who attempt to describe cultures to distinguish clearly between the culture constructs which they themselves have developed on the basis of observation and the ideal culture patterns which have been transmitted to them verbally by members of the society, no matter how honestly or with what good intentions.

Readers whose main interests lie in the field of personality psychology may feel that undue space has been devoted to this analysis of the culture concept. Much of what has been said admittedly has little bearing on investigations carried on within the limits of our own society and culture. Here the patterns of normal behavior are so well known to the investigator, and deviations from them so readily recognizable, that there is little need for abstracting or conceptualizing them. However, as soon as investigations are extended beyond this relatively narrow field, an understanding of culture concepts becomes a necessity.

3

Social Structure and Culture Participation

It has been emphasized in previous chapters that societies rather than individuals are the functional units in our species' struggle for existence and that it is societies as wholes which are the bearers and perpetuators of cultures. It has also been pointed out that no one individual is ever familiar with the total culture of his society, still less required to express all its manifold patterns in his overt behavior. However, the participation of any given individual in the culture of his society is not a matter of chance. It is determined primarily, and almost completely as far as the overt culture is concerned, by his place in the society and by the training which he has received in anticipation of his occupying this place. It follows that the behavior of the individual must be studied not simply in relation to the total culture of his society but also in relation to the particular cultural demands which his society makes upon him because of his place in it. Thus all societies expect different behavior from men and from women, and one cannot understand the behavior of any particular man or woman without knowing what these expectations are.

Most present-day investigators of personality are perfectly cognizant of these facts and of the desirability of gaining a clear picture of the structure of a society as a preliminary to determining the social-cultural environments of its members. At the same time, I believe that it is fair to say that most of them find it difficult to utilize for this purpose the material presented in most sociological studies. Much of the difficulty seems to be due to the failure of many sociologists to distinguish clearly between a society and its culture. A society is an organized group of people, a collection of individuals who have learned to work together. A culture is an organized group of behavior patterns, and so forth. Although the interrelations of a society and its culture are close and numerous, the two things are distinct and represent phenomena of different orders. In spite of this, many sociologists describe societies in terms of institutions and use the term *social structure* to refer to the interrelations of institutions. Actually, an institution is a configuration of culture patterns which, as a whole, has certain functions; and the interrelations of such configurations belong primarily to the areas of culture organization or integration. The institutional approach to society, although useful for certain purposes, tends to ignore the relation between institutions and individuals. In many cases it is impossible to tell from descriptions developed on this basis what sort of people participate in a particular institution or to place any given member of the society with relation to it. To be of use to students of personality, formulations of social structure must begin at the other end of the social-cultural configuration. They must show how the individuals who compose the society are classified and organized, since it is through these mechanisms that the society's members, as individuals, are assigned their rôles in the corporate existence of the society.

The first step in developing formulations of social structure which will be of use in personality studies is that of determining what sort of social units are primarily responsible for establishing the individual's participation in culture. The term *society* has been applied to a great variety of human groupings, varying all the way from business men's luncheon clubs to the American Commonwealth. However, many of such organized groups are strictly limited in their aims and their claims upon the individual. Although they may function with respect to the operation and perpetuation of a few elements within a culture, they do not employ or transmit cultures as wholes. We will limit our discussion, therefore, to the sort of organized groupings which can function as independent culture bearers. Furthermore, we will begin with the simplest and most universal form of such culture-bearing groups, since it is in this that the principles underlying all social structure are most readily discernible.

All human beings normally live as members of a society which is composed of individuals of both sexes and all ages and which perpetuates itself by producing children and then training them to take their places as functioning members of the organization. Although one other type of organized grouping, the family, may be even older, this sort of society certainly goes back to the beginnings of our existence as a distinct species.

Both it and the family are to be found wherever men live. The members of such a society are united by a multitude of common interests and a strong consciousness of kind based upon personal acquaintance and personal interaction. They stand as a unit against outsiders and divide the activities necessary to the wellbeing of the group among themselves according to a definite pattern. This pattern assures that all members of the group shall both contribute services and receive benefits. Lastly, in spite of the differences in behavior entailed by different rôles, all members of the society share a long series of culture patterns, especially covert patterns, and recognize a common value system. It is the transmission of this completely shared nucleus of culture which provides the members of the society with common understandings and which makes it possible for the society, as such, to survive repeated turnovers in its personnel.

It is an exceedingly significant fact that even these simplest, primary societies are not completely amorphous in their structure. They are configurations not only of individuals but also of smaller, internally organized groups of individuals. Human beings appear to have an urgent need for the emotional security to be derived from close and extensive adjustments to a few other individuals. They also have great ability for coöperating toward the achievement of limited, specific goals and for integrating themselves into functional units. Even within the simplest societies we find friendships and work groups which set off small numbers of persons, usually of the same sex and approximate age, from the rest of the society and establish relations of a particular type among them. We also find family groupings which unite a small series of individuals of both sexes and all ages into closely integrated units. The membership of the individual in such a unit, especially if it be a family group, is a significant factor in orienting him with respect to the society and its culture. While it provides him with special satisfactions, it also entails special obligations both in terms of joint responsibility to the larger society and of the reciprocal rights and duties existing between the members of the unit. Thus a man derives numerous personal advantages from marrying and setting up a family of his own, but he also makes himself legally responsible for his wife's debts and for damage caused by his children and assumes special obligations toward the wife and children.

This pattern of what might be termed cellular organization manifests itself throughout the whole range of social integrations. Every society from the primitive band to the modern state is really an organized aggregate of smaller organized groups. Thus the band is a configuration of family, friendship and work groupings, the tribe a configuration of bands, the state, in its simpler forms, a configuration of tribes which have been brought together by conquest or confederation, and so forth. Except for occasional periods of disintegration and confusion, this principle of organization can be recognized in even the most complex modern societies. Moreover, such periods of confusion are always transitory. Thus in a newly founded war industry town there are, at first, no social configurations intervening between the migratory workman and the local society as a whole, but as time goes on such configurations are sure to develop. Affiliations with unions, lodges, churches, and so on, will serve to set off certain series of individuals from the society as a whole, bring them together and provide them with opportunities for integrating themselves into functioning social units.

In more stabilized modern societies the functions of the simple primary society with respect both to the integration of individuals and the transmission of culture are performed primarily by local communities and social classes. Even in such a society as our own, no two communities have identical cultures. Beneath the superficial similarities due to mass production and such agencies as the movies and radio there are frequently significant differences in attitudes and values. Social classes may also function as primary societies within the larger configuration, especially when they are of long standing and with clearly defined membership. Each class tends to develop its own set of shared and transmitted culture patterns and to establish certain special obligations among its members. It also tends to preëmpt for its members and to make a part of its distinctive culture certain activities necessary to the survival of the larger configuration. Thus in European societies men of the upper classes are expected to assume leadership in war, and physical cowardice is much more severely reprehended in them than in men of lower class.

Interestingly enough, the existence of primary societies delimited on a class basis is by no means incompatible with a considerable degree of individual mobility within the class structure. The main requirement for the persistence of a class society seems to be that it shall have a fair measure of internal organization and a well-defined, distinctive culture. In all societies the first step taken by a person seeking acceptance into a higher class is to assume the overt culture patterns of that class and to abandon those of his own. In England, which someone has said is the last place in the world where "gentleman" means something as concrete as "sausage," there are even special techniques for the acculturation to upper-class patterns of persons of lower-class birth. The individual who has acquired enough wealth to maintain upper-class status frequently cannot assume the distinctive patterns of the upper-class successfully. In order to do so he will have to change even his linguistic behavior. However, he can send his son to a public school (something quite different from what the American means by this term) from which the boy will emerge culturally indistinguishable from other boys with a long upper-class ancestry.

All primary societies, irrespective of whether they stand alone or function as units in larger integrations, have certain features of organization in common. All of them divide their membership into various categories based on differences in age and sex. All of them differentiate certain individuals or groups of individuals from the rest of the society on the basis of specialized occupations. All of them include within their organization smaller, internally organized units of two sorts: (1) family groups, membership in which is established on the basis of biological relationships, real or assumed, and (2) association groups, membership in which is established on the basis of congeniality and/or common interest. Lastly, all societies tend to arrange both their individual members and the units established by these various systems of organization in prestige series, according greater social importance, and consequently influence, to certain units within each series than to others. Certain primary societies may amplify these basic systems of organization in various ways. Thus most Polynesian groups accord high prestige to first-born children irrespective of sex and ascribe special social functions to them. However, most of the organization of any primary society can be analysed and described in terms of the basic structural patterns just listed.

In the case of social configurations including several primary societies the structuring becomes more complicated, but the same basic principles remain in force. The primary societies retain their independent structures, but new structural patterns, oriented upon the larger configuration, are superimposed. Membership in the various units established by this all-over organization cuts across the lines of the primary societies and the units themselves assume integrative functions with respect to the larger configuration as a whole. Thus the fact that a war party, or secret society, or extended kin group includes individuals from several different primary societies serves to draw these societies together and aids them in functioning as integral parts of the larger whole.

In the development of all-over patterns of organization there seems to be a strong tendency to project the organizational systems of the primary societies upon the larger grouping. In certain cases, such as the creation of the League of the Iroquois, this seems to have been done consciously and deliberately. In most cases, however, it is probably unconscious, an attempt to apply familiar patterns to situations which resemble in certain respects those with relation to which these patterns have been employed. Thus in almost every case a clan organization which cuts across the primary society lines within a tribe will be found to be correlated in many of its features with the family organization existing within these societies. The criteria of clan membership will normally represent extensions of the kin concepts which are basic to family membership; the same relationship terms, within limits, will be applied to clan and family members; and the reciprocal rights and duties of clan members will be closely patterned upon those of family members, although the obligations will be somewhat diluted. Any associative groupings which cut across primary society lines will also be found, in most cases, to agree closely in both purpose and patterns of organization with those existing within the primary societies. Lastly, the various communities or classes incorporated into the larger society will normally be arranged in a prestige series and will exercise greater or less influence in the formulation of the society's policies according to their positions in this series.

Reverting to the features always present in the structure of primary societies, the division of the society's members into age-sex categories is, perhaps, the feature of greatest importance for establishing the participation of the individual in culture. In practically all societies the great majority of activities and occupations are ascribed to the members of one or a very small number of age-sex categories and prohibited to members of others. Even in the case of highly specialized activities which may themselves be used as a basis for distinguishing certain groups of individuals from the society in general, membership in a particular age-sex category is usually a prerequisite for full participation in such activities. Thus in the community in which I spent my childhood, only middle-aged or old men were regarded as reliable medical practitioners. Young doctors fresh from medical school were viewed with suspicion and always tried to make themselves look older than they were. One of my acquaintances, who had become bald in his early twenties, told me that this was one of the most valuable items in his professional equipment. Such specialist groups differ from the corresponding age-sex categories both in their technical equipment and in their much smaller membership. Thus in our own society all plumbers are adult males, but all adult males are not plumbers. Nearly all stenographers, except court stenographers, are women, but all women are not stenographers.

In addition to prescribing occupations and activities, membership in a particular age-sex group immediately provides the individual with a long series of patterns for the behavior proper in his relations with members of other age-sex groups. These patterns hold good whether he knows the other individuals involved or not. It is only necessary for him to recognize the category to which another person belongs for him to know how to behave toward the other and the sort of behavior he is entitled to expect in return. Lastly, there is also a universal tendency to ascribe different participations in the covert culture of the society to members of different age-sex categories. They are expected not only to possess different sorts of knowledge but also to have differing value attitude systems. Thus in our own society men are supposed to know more about machinery than women, a natural outgrowth of certain of the occupations in which they commonly engage. However, in at least the lower levels of our society, they are also supposed to be better judges of meat and better able to pick a prime roast or steak at the butcher shop. Common sense suggests that women, who do most of the shopping, are in a better position to recognize good meat, and this ascription of special knowledge to men seems to be a carry-over from the former rural conditions in which men did their own butchering on the farm. As regards value attitude systems, we have such things as the use of the term *childish* to designate both certain interests and certain patterns of emotional response and our deep-seated belief that women are innately gentler and less aggressive than men in spite of frequent experience to the contrary.

The division of a society's members into age-sex categories must be regarded as primarily a taxonomic device. The groupings thus established are in no sense organized, functional units, although the members of a particular category may be capable of concerted action when they realize that their common interests are threatened. Most teachers and parents can remember examples of the group solidarity of which children are capable under certain circumstances. *Lysistrata* also comes to mind at this point, but those who remember the play will also remember how rapidly the category organization broke down when it came into conflict with the individual interests of the group's members.

The starting point for age-sex classification and the practical justification for it lie in the differing potentialities of males and females at various age levels. Obviously, the average man is stronger than the average boy and can do certain things which the boy cannot. It is equally clear that the adult female has certain potentialities in connection with reproduction and infant care not shared by the members of any other category. Nevertheless, we find that even the age-sex categories recognized by all societies reflect more than simple biology. A minimum of seven age-sex categories is recognized everywhere. These are: infant, boy, girl, adult male, adult female, old male, old female. Actually, pre-pubertal boys and girls differ very little in strength and activity and would be quite capable of participating in nearly all of the same culture patterns. The distinction which is everywhere made between them is due to their anticipated differences as adults. The boy is trained for his rôle as a man and the girl for hers as a woman. Similarly, old men and old women are not very different in their physical potentialities. In fact old women are often stronger and more active than men of the same age. However, each sex has spent a lifetime in special training and in the exercise of the particular skills ascribed to it in the society's division of labor. Individuals have learned to act as men or as women and continue to do so to the end. It may be worth noting in this connection that there are many societies in which the distinction between male and female rôles does become less pronounced for women after the menopause. Old women are often allowed to take an active part in ceremonies and religious practices which were previously taboo to them and to assume positions of dominance and control within family groups closely paralleling those held by men at the lower age levels.

Although the seven categories just mentioned are recognized by all societies, many societies amplify the series in various ways. Each of the main categories is susceptible of numerous subdivisions, while adolescents may or may not be recognized as a distinct group with a right to their own culture patterns. Adolescents are distinct in certain physiological respects from both children and adults, and the techniques which various societies have developed for dealing with them are of considerable interest to students of personality, especially in view of the poor success which attends our own efforts along this line. In societies which recognize adolescents as a distinct category and ascribe to them activities suited to their condition, the period passes with little or no stress and the transition from the rôles of childhood to those of adult life is accomplished with little shock to the personality. Societies which choose to ignore the particular qualities of adolescence may elect to deal with the situation in either of two ways. They may extend the child category, with its ascribed attitudes and patterns of overt behavior, upward to include adolescents, or they may project the adult category downward to include them. In either case the adolescent becomes a problem for himself and for others. If he is expected to adhere to childhood patterns of obedience and dependence, he either becomes a bad child, in revolt against authority, or he submits and establishes these patterns in himself so firmly that he experiences great difficulty in assuming adult responsibilities and initiative when the time comes. If he is expected to follow adult patterns from the moment of puberty, he finds himself called upon to assume forms of behavior which tax his abilities to the uttermost even when they do not exceed them. Although the society may formally class him as a man, he remains for a long time a second-rate one, inferior to most other members of the category and consequently subject to all sorts of frustrations. Perhaps the one thing worse than either of these methods is to do as we do and leave the social rôle of adolescents in doubt. We alternately demand from them the obedience and submission of children and the initiative and acceptance of personal responsibilities which go with adult status. The results of this inconsistent treatment are too well known to students of personality psychology to require discussion.

The ascription of particular culture patterns to individuals on the basis of their specialized occupations is generally of a rather limited sort. It cannot compare in extent with that based on membership in particular age-sex groups, and the patterns thus ascribed are usually minor extensions or amplifications of those which belong to the age-sex category with which the specialized occupation is linked. Although such occupational patterns necessarily include the skills and knowledge connected with the specialty, they need not be confined to these. Thus, to cite one of the most frequent cases, workers with the supernatural are usually distinguished from the rest of their age-sex category by prescribed patterns of costume and behavior which they are expected to follow even when not engaged in their special occupation. Everyone in our own society knows the meaning of the reversed collar, and most Protestant sects feel that it is improper for a pastor to smoke or drink even in moderation and when off duty. Certain attitudes and personality characteristics may also be ascribed to individuals on the basis of their special occupations. Such ascriptions are in the nature of ideal culture patterns and may bear little relation to reality, yet they are frequently reflected in the behavior of others toward such specialists. Thus our own ancestors assumed that all butchers were callous and bloodthirsty individuals, and in many communities they, together with physicians, were forbidden to sit on juries in cases involving the death penalty. Again, the cowardice of tailors is a stock motif in North European folklore. Any of my readers who were raised on *Grimm's Fairy Tales,* some of which are grim enough, will remember the little tailor in "Seven at One Stroke."

Such ascriptions are not of great importance to studies of the individual in the so-called primitive societies. In these the forms of specialization are few and the number of specialists small. However, occupational specialization increases rapidly with increasing complexity of culture, reaching a peak in such civilizations as our own. Under these conditions the behavior patterns and attitudes ascribed to specialists of a particular sort may play an important rôle in the selection of a particular specialized occupation by the individual. This is, of course, linked with the considerable freedom of choice of occupations which is also characteristic of our society at this time. The man who feels that he would be most content as a longshoreman or a bookkeeper still has an excellent chance of becoming either one. However, in cases where the individual is not permitted to make such a choice, the behavior and attitudes ascribed to members of the specialist group in which he finds himself may be quite uncongenial and frequently are a cause of maladjustment and psychological disturbance. Thus the son of one eminent professor of the writer's acquaintance, who had been pushed and pulled into an academic post, finally found the requirements of his university position so oppressive that he disappeared in the middle of a term.

Membership in family groupings is usually of little importance for determining the individual's occupations, although it is not infrequent for special crafts, particularly those which are lucrative and involve trade secrets, to be transmitted in family lines. The work ascribed to different individuals in the division of activities within the family seems to be controlled primarily by their age and sex rather than by their position in the family structure. Family membership is also of minor importance in determining the overt behavior of family members to persons outside the group except when it relates to particular individuals or members of other families with which the first family has established special relationships of friendliness or enmity. It does, however, provide a basis for the ascription of certain attitudes toward outsiders in general, especially that their interests shall be considered secondary to those of family members. Lastly, in societies which have patterns of joint responsibility for the acts of any family member it may impose special behaviors upon the individual.

All these aspects of culture ascription are rather incidental as far as family organization is concerned. The main ascriptive function of the family is that of providing the individual with patterns for his behavior toward other individuals within the family group. These other individuals are formally classified on the basis of their biological or marital relationships to him, with the ascription of particular rights and duties with respect to the members of each class. The systems of classification and the patterns of behavior prescribed for interaction with the members of each class of relatives may vary greatly from one society to another. Describing and classifying relationship systems has been one of the favorite sports of anthropologists since the inception of the science, and the literature already available on the subject is voluminous. However, the differences between systems are of little significance for our present discussion. The important thing for us is that numerous culture patterns relating to social interaction are ascribed to the individual on the basis of family membership and that the particular individuals toward whom these patterns should be exercised are clearly designated on the same basis. Since the individuals standing in any one relationship are strictly limited in number, and contacts with them are usually close and frequent, the family situation is one in which culturally ascribed patterns are particularly susceptible to modification through experience. In other words, the individual has plenty of opportunity to know his relatives as people and to adjust his behavior toward them in terms of his and their personalities. Although it cannot be proved on the basis of our present knowledge, it seems highly probable that the behavior included within the real culture patterns corresponding to relationship situations is more variable than that existing with respect to any others. Nevertheless, this is also one of the areas in which societies are most likely to develop ideal patterns and in which public departure from these patterns is most severely reprehended. It follows that in the study of individual personalities and their social environments the investigator must take into account the private as well as the public behavior of family members toward one another. Many a man who has made a social faux pas has spent the rest of the evening cringing at the prospect of what his ostentatiously devoted and sympathetic wife will say when they get home.

Association groups differ from family groups in two important respects. Their membership is usually confined to individuals of the same sex and somewhere near the same age, and entry into such groups is more or less voluntary. Exceptions can be found to both of these rules in various societies, but they hold good in the great majority of cases. Such groupings are formed on the basis of congeniality or common interest but usually involve elements of both. Thus even in work groups whose avowed purposes are strictly practical and economic, some care will usually be taken to include only individuals who are sufficiently congenial to be able to coöperate with a minimum of friction. Such association groups include units of many sorts. Friendships and cliques belong in this class, as do work groups, clubs and societies in the ordinary usage of the term. Even the most informal of such groupings have some measure of internal organization, while those of any sort may be highly organized in certain societies. Thus in Dahomey the friend relationship involves rights and duties quite as specific as those existing between close relatives of any particular sort, say brothers. In the case of larger groupings, such as clubs or secret societies, the organization may be elaborate and formal, with officers and special rituals. Membership in such a unit always results in the ascription to the individual of certain patterns of behavior toward other members. It may also result, especially if the unit has certain functions with respect to the society as a whole, in the ascription of special behavior toward outsiders. Such behavior is usually of a sporadic sort. The individual is expected to adhere to it only while the association group is engaged in its ceremonies or in the performance of its special functions. Thus the members of a Plains Indian Men's Society will be expected to behave in certain ways while the society is giving its dance or exercising police functions, but to behave like anyone else at other times.

Lastly, the ranging of individuals and groups in prestige series may be linked with the formal ascription of different forms of behavior to persons occupying different positions in such a series. Even in societies which lack a true class structure with its associated differences in culture patterns, there is usually a feeling that individuals of high prestige should behave in certain ways. This is reflected in our own familiar phrase, "Noblesse oblige." Such persons are usually expected to be chary in the exercise of their real power and considerate of those below them, and failure in this results in loss of esteem. Even when no formal patterns of behavior are linked to positions in the prestige series, such positions inevitably influence the behavior of individuals within the range of variation set by real culture patterns. Everyone acts somewhat differently toward superiors, equals and inferiors, and even if the overt behavior toward a person in one of these relationships is the same as that normal toward persons in another, the effects produced will be different. Thus an inferior is flattered to be treated like an equal, a superior irritated by it.

In summary, each of the systems of classification and organization existing within a primary society ascribes certain culture patterns to the individual on the basis of his position in the system. However, the systems are of varying importance in this respect. The individual's position in the age-sex system apparently does more than any other to determine his participation in culture. Next in importance comes his position in the family system, although the main significance of this is to provide him with patterns governing his relations with a limited, specific group of other individuals rather than with the society as a whole. His positions in the systems of specialized activities, association groups and prestige ratings also operate in the ascription of culture patterns, but in this respect none of these systems appear to be anything like as important as the first two. The investigator who can establish his subject's place in the age-sex categories and the family system can deduce from these the bulk of his cultural participation, at least with respect to the particular point in time at which the investigation is made. Moreover it will always be possible to set up groups of individuals who belong to the same age-sex category and who occupy similar positions within various family units. The culture participation common to the members of such groups provides something as near to a stable frame of reference as can be found under the conditions in which all personality studies must still be made. Individual variations in behavior and response can be studied and compared in relation to it, and the causes of these variations can be investigated.

Up to this point we have been dealing with culture participation in the general, impersonal terms of social structure. We must turn now to the individual in his relation to this structure and, through it, to the culture of his society. It should be clear by this time that the structure of even the simplest primary society, such as a primitive village, is by no means simple or homogeneous. The individuals who compose such a society are classified and organized in several different ways simultaneously. Each of these systems has its own functions as regards relating the individual to culture, and he occupies a place within each of them. Thus every member of the society has a place in the age-sex system and also in the prestige series. He has a place in the system of specialized occupations, either as a specialist or as a member of the unassigned residue which, in our own society, is designated by such vague terms as *unskilled laborer* or *housewife*. Lastly, he always belongs to some family unit and to one or more association groups. As long as he has a single living relative within the society, he has position in the family system; and even if all his kindred have been swept away, he can reënter the system by the road of adoption or marriage. As regards membership in the system based on association, any member of a primary society who is not psychotic can hardly fail to be included in friendship units and work groups. He may be debarred from belonging to clubs or other of the more formal association groupings, but even so he occupies a very definite place in the system of which such groups are a part. He is one of the "outsiders," and it is the presence of this group which provides the "members" with most of their emotional satisfaction. It is inconceivable that a secret society could exist without a large audience of nonmembers to envy the members and speculate about the secrets.

In past attempts to clarify the relation of the individual to these multiple social systems, two terms have proved so useful that it seems justifiable to introduce them here. We have tried to make it clear that the systems persist while the individuals who occupy places within them may come and go. The place in a particular system which a certain individual occupies at a particular time will be referred to as his *status* with respect to that system. The term *position* has been used by some other students of social structure in much the same sense, but without clear recognition of the time factor or of the existence of simultaneous systems of organization within the society. *Status* has long been used with reference to the position of an individual in the prestige system of his society. In the present usage this is extended to apply to his position in each of the other systems. The second term, *rôle,* will be used to designate the sum total of the culture patterns associated with a particular status. It thus includes the attitudes, values and behavior ascribed by the society to any and all persons occupying this status. It can even be extended to include the legitimate expectations of such persons with respect to the behavior toward them of persons in other statuses within the same system. Every status is linked with a particular rôle, but the two things are by no means the same from the point of view of the individual. His statuses are ascribed to him on the basis of his age and sex, his birth or marriage into a particular family unit, and so forth. His rôles are learned on the basis of his statuses, either current or anticipated. In so far as it represents overt behavior, a rôle is the dynamic aspect of a status: what the individual has to do in order to validate his occupation of the status.

A particular status within a social system can be occupied, and its associated rôle known and exercised, by a number of individuals simultaneously. In fact, this is the normal condition. Thus every society ordinarily includes several persons who occupy the status of adult male and adhere to the adult male rôle. It similarly includes a number of persons who occupy the status of father in the organizations of the particular family groups to which they belong. Conversely, the same individual can and does occupy simultaneously a series of statuses each of which derives from one of the systems of organization in which he participates. He not only occupies these statuses, but he also knows the rôles pertaining to them. However, he can never exercise all these rôles simultaneously. Such rôles are a constant element in his participation in the covert culture of his society, but function intermittently with respect to his participation in its overt culture. In other words, although he occupies statuses and knows rôles at all times, he operates sometimes in terms of one status and its rôle, sometimes in those of another. The status in terms of which an individual is operating is his *active status* at that particular point in time. His other statuses are, for the time being, *latent statuses*. The rôles associated with such latent statuses are temporarily held in abeyance, but they are integral parts of the individual's culture equipment.

This formulation can be made clearer by an example. Let us suppose that a man spends the day working as clerk in a store. While he is behind the counter, his active status is that of a clerk, established by his position in our society's system of specialized occupations. The rôle associated with this status provides him with patterns for his relations with customers. These patterns will be well known both to him and to the customers and will enable them to transact business with a minimum of delay or misunderstanding. When he retires to the rest room for a smoke and meets other employees there, his clerk status becomes latent and he assumes another active status based upon his position in the association group composed of the store's employees as a whole. In this status his relations with other employees will be governed by a different set of culture patterns from those employed in his relations with customers. Moreover, since he probably knows most of the other employees, his exercise of these culture patterns will be modified by his personal likes and dislikes of certain individuals and by considerations of their and his own relative positions in the prestige series of the store association's members. When closing times comes, he lays aside both his clerk and store association statuses and, while on the way home, operates simply in terms of his status with respect to the society's age-sex system. Thus if he is a young man he will at least feel that he ought to get up and give his seat to a lady, while if he is an old one he will be quite comfortable about keeping it. As soon as he arrives at his house, a new set of statuses will be activated. These statuses derive from the kinship ties which relate him to various members of the family group. In pursuance of the rôles associated with these family statuses he will try to be cordial to his mother-in-law, affectionate to his wife and a stern disciplinarian to Junior, whose report card marks a new low. If it happens to be lodge night, all his familial statuses will become latent at about eight o'clock. As soon as he enters the lodge room and puts on his uniform as Grand Imperial Lizzard, in the Ancient Order of Dinosaurs he assumes a new status, one which has been latent since the last lodge meeting, and performs in terms of its rôle until it is time for him to take off his uniform and go home.

The fact that the individual's various statuses are activated at different times prevents a head-on collision between the rôles associated with them. At most, the overt behavior which is part of the rôle connected with one status may negate the results of the overt behavior which is part of another rôle. The behaviors themselves will not conflict because of the time differential. Moreover, the rôles associated with the statuses within a single system are usually fairly well adjusted to one another and produce no conflicts as long as the individual is operating within this system. This also holds for statuses within different systems whenever these statuses are of such a sort that they normally converge upon the same individuals. Thus in any society the rôles of adult male, of father, of craft specialist, of friend, and so on, will normally be adjusted to one another in spite of the different systems from which they derive. Such adjustments, of course, are not the result of conscious planning. They are developed through the experience of individuals who have occupied such series of statuses simultaneously and have gradually eliminated most of the conflicts through a process of trial and error. Thus if patterns of formal friendship are borrowed from some other society, such patterns will soon be modified in such ways that there will be no conflict between them and the patterns already established by the local system of family organization.

In the rare cases in which, through some accident, statuses whose rôles are fundamentally incompatible converge upon the same individual, we have the material of high tragedy. While most societies feel little sympathy for the individual who is trying to escape the performance of certain of his rôles, all can sympathize with the dilemma of a person who must choose between statuses and rôles which are equally valid. Such dilemmas are a favorite theme in the literature of the more sophisticated or introspective societies. The tragedy of the House of Oedipus and the closing episodes of the Niebelungenlied are classical examples, while at the level of simpler folklore we have the Scottish story of the man who finds himself host to his brother's murderer. In each of these cases the individual upon whom the incompatible rôles converge meets the problem by the familiar pattern of operating in terms of different statuses at different times, even though recognizing that the associated rôles will, in their performance, negate each other's results. Thus in the Scottish story the brother, as host, conducts the murderer safely beyond clan territory then, as brother to the victim, engages him in combat to the death.

Such conflicts rarely arise in primary societies or even within larger social groupings which have persisted for some time and developed well-integrated cultures. However, they may become fairly frequent under the conditions existing in our current society. Under the necessity of reorganizing our social structure to meet the needs of a new technology and of a spatial mobility unparalleled in human history, our inherited system of statuses and rôles is breaking down; while a new system, compatible with the actual conditions of modern life, has not yet emerged. The individual thus finds himself frequently confronted by situations in which he is uncertain both of his own statuses and rôles and of those of others. He is not only compelled to make choices but also can feel no certainty that he has chosen correctly and that the reciprocal behavior of others will be that which he anticipates on the basis of the statuses which he has assumed that they occupy. This results in numerous disappointments and frustrations.

4

Personality

RECOGNITION of the phenomena which are the sub matter of personality studies must be as old as species. Even the ape man soon learned by experi that certain members of the horde were good nat or irascible, stupid or intelligent, stolid or quick emotional response. However, throughout most c man history such differences have been regarded as in the nature of things, requiring no explanation. The emergence of modern concepts of personality and the study of the process involved in personality formation are exceedingly recent developments. They are even newer than the studies of culture and society some of whose results have been presented in the previous chapters. It is not surprising, therefore, that considerable confusion still exists with regard to the concepts and definitions which must be used as tools in personality studies. Even the exact meaning to be given to the term personality is still unsettled. There are innumerable definitions extant, all of which have certain elements in common, but the process of clarification through usage, already described in connection with the definition of culture, is still under way.

Actually, the main problem involved in the definition of personality is one of delimitation. The individual and his environment constitute a dynamic configuration all of whose parts are so closely interrelated and in such constant interaction that it is very hard to tell where to draw lines of demarkation. For the purpose of the present discussion, personality will be taken to mean: "The organized aggregate of psychological processes and states pertaining to the individual." This definition includes the common element in most of the definitions now current. At the same time it excludes many orders of phenomena which have been included in one or another of these definitions. Thus it rules out the overt behavior resulting from the operation of these processes and states, although it is only from such behavior that their nature and even existence can be deduced. It also excludes from consideration the effects of this behavior upon the individual's environment, even that part of it which consists of other individuals. Lastly, it excludes from the personality concept the physical structure of the individual and his physiological processes. This final limitation will appear too drastic to many students of personality, but it has a pragmatic, if not a logical, justification. We know so little about the physiological accompaniments of psychological phenomena that attempts to deal with the latter in physiological terms still lead to more confusion than clarification. In the face of a universe all of whose parts are in some degree interrelated, all sciences set arbitrary limits to their fields of research. Experience has shown that it is possible to arrive at valid conclusions about phenomena of a particular order without reference to all the phenomena of other orders with which those of the first order may be functionally interrelated. Thus the geneticists have been able to establish their laws of heredity without reference to the gene chemistry upon which the reproduction of physical characteristics must ultimately depend. Similarly, experimental psychologists have been able to find out a great deal about the learning processes by dealing with them in purely psychological and behavioral terms, although they are still almost completely ignorant of the physiological accompaniments of these processes.

The phrase *psychological processes and states* is admittedly vague, and it seems wiser to leave it so. We probably know less about the actual content and structure of personality than about any other aspect of the individual. Personalities are configurations of a unique sort, one which has no close parallel at the level of physical phenomena. Moreover, they are not susceptible to direct observation. We can only deduce their qualities from the overt behavior in which these qualities find expression. Going a step farther, the only grounds for assuming the existence of personalities as operative entities persisting through time is the consistency in the overt behavior of individuals. The individual's repetition of similar responses to similar stimuli, in those cases where such responses are complex and obviously not instinctual, can only be accounted for on the assumption that experience is, in some way, organized and perpetuated. Unfortunately, observed behavior is often susceptible of more than one psychological interpretation. It follows that any one of several different formulations of personality content and structure can take care of the bulk of the known facts. To add to the confusion, most of the attempts to describe personality involve the use of terms drawn from the more familiar field of physical phenomena and scarcely applicable to psychological ones. Thus, to speak of levels within the personality evokes an image of spatial relationships which by no means corresponds to the varying degrees of integration, of susceptibility to change or of availability to introspective or logical approaches which the psychologist means by the term. It is not surprising, therefore, that many of the current chartings of personality are reminiscent of seventeenth-century maps. The coast lines are clear enough, but the blankness of the interior is masked by sketches of the hairy, ithyphallic Id, the haloed Superego, and the inscription: *"Hereabouts there be complexes."*

Since our only clues to personality are those provided by the overt behavior of the individual and the apparent relations of this behavior to his needs and his environment, it seems justifiable to approach the problem of formulating personality content from a functional standpoint. We may take as our first premise that the function of the personality as a whole is to enable the individual to produce forms of behavior which will be advantageous to him under the conditions imposed by his environment. We will then take as our second premise that, other things being equal, this function is performed most effectively when the advantageous behavior is produced with a minimum of delay and involves a minimum of effort. The conditions of the second premise are met most successfully by those automatic responses of tested effectiveness which we term habits. On the basis of these two premises, the operation of the personality may be summed up as:

1. The development of adequate behavioral responses to various situations
2. The reduction of these responses to habitual terms
3. The production of the habitual responses already established

In all three of these operations the initial step is the *registry* [1] of the situation which evokes the response. I have chosen to use this term rather than *recognition* or *perception* because both of these carry connotations of consciousness. When a situation is new or unfamiliar its registry will tend to be at the conscious level, but once it has become familiar and is linked with an adequate habitual response, its registry may be quite unconscious. Thus an individual may register several situations and produce the habitual responses to them as they arise without knowing that he has done so and without interrupting the flow of his conscious psychological processes. Registry of this sort is a necessary preliminary to response, whether the situation involved derives primarily from internal or external factors. Thus most people who engage in creative work know that the physiological tensions created by hunger or fatigue may fail to register over long periods, asserting themselves only when a lull comes in the creative activity. The vigor with which they assert themselves at

[1] This term was first used with this meaning by Dr. Karen Horney.

such times is sufficient proof that the tensions themselves have followed their normal course of development; it is only their registry as stimuli that has been blocked. That the registry of stimuli originating outside the organism is a necessary preliminary to response is too obvious to require discussion. One does not jump out of the way of an auto unless one sees it coming.

In the above formulation of the first step in the development of a stimulus-response sequence, the term *situation* has been used deliberately and in preference to the more precise and limited term *stimulus*. Practically all the situations which evoke responses in human beings involve multiple factors. Psychologists who approach the study of human behavior with a background of laboratory experimentation on animals are prone to underrate the extreme complexity of the conditions under which most of man's behavior is developed and carried out. The needs of the individual, which must be regarded as the ultimate motivations of behavior, rarely function as isolated stimuli, since most of them are present most of the time. This situation is exaggerated by the human ability to foresee the recurrence of needs even when they are currently at a low level of intensity. Thus for men on a raft present hunger and anticipated hunger operate as stimuli of almost equal importance in determining the way in which their limited food supply is to be used. Even without this factor of anticipation, it is quite possible for several needs to register with the individual simultaneously. Thus any former Boy Scout knows that one can be at the same time hungry, cold, tired and anxious

PERSONALITY 89

to make a good impression on one's companions. The needs which are present at any given moment differ in their urgency. If the satisfaction of any one of them, especially of a need based on physiological tensions, is delayed too long, it may come to dominate the situation and to operate as the exclusive motivation of behavior. However, this situation rarely arises under the normal conditions of human existence. What usually happens is that several needs, none of which are strongly dominant, operate together to provide the motivation for a particular behavioral response. This response, in turn, is designed to satisfy all the needs involved in greater or less degree. Thus, to revert to the Boy Scout example, the combined needs for food, warmth, rest and for maintaining the good opinion of other members of the troop will result in an attempt to persuade the whole group to head for home.

Further complications are introduced by the fact that any behavior which will suffice to satisfy a particular need or aggregate of needs must be organized in terms of the conditions established by the individual's environment. Although the registry of a need may precede the individual's appraisal of these conditions, both are necessary preliminaries to the development of effective behavioral responses. While the two may be separated analytically, it is an open question whether they can be separated functionally. Especially in the case of established behavioral responses, that is, habits, there seems to be abundant evidence that a need or aggregate of needs and the conditions under which it normally finds satisfaction function as a single stimulus unit. Moreover, in many cases recognition of the conditions seems to be enough to set in train the habitual response even when the needs involved in the configuration would not register in the absence of these conditions. Thus it is a common experience that a tempting meal will awaken appetite and lead to the habitual eating responses even when there has been no previous feeling of hunger. It seems probable that in such cases the needs involved in the stimulus situation are actually present when the conditions are recognized but are being held in abeyance. Although the needs of the individual vary in intensity from moment to moment, under the normal conditions of living it is unusual for any need to be completely satisfied. Even when the tension basic to a particular need has been reduced below the point at which it would normally function as an initiator of behavior, there is enough residual tension to enable the need to function as a motivator of behavior when the familiar conditions are present. When an habitual response serves to satisfy several needs simultaneously, the sum of the residual tensions of these needs is presumably enough to set the behavior in train.

The situations which may evoke behavioral responses are exceedingly numerous and variable. They include most of the possible permutations and combinations of the individual's needs and of the various conditions under which these needs may be satisfied. However there is at least one factor, which we will call the *social component,* which is common to the great majority of human stimulus situations. This social component derives from the conditions implicit in existence as a member of an organized group and from the individual's thorough habituation to these conditions. As has already been said, most human patterns of behavior are responses not to a single need but to an aggregate of needs. The need for eliciting favorable responses from others is an almost constant component of such aggregates. Indeed, it is not too much to say that there is very little organized human behavior which is not directed toward its satisfaction in at least some degree. Although this need for response probably varies in intensity at different times, it lacks the clear-cut cyclical quality of those needs which derive directly from physiological tensions. It can thus operate as a motivation of behavior at almost any time. It is hard to conceive of a situation in which the individual's desire for favorable response from others is so completely satisfied that he has no desire to elicit further favorable responses or to avoid unfavorable ones.

Since other individuals are an almost constant element in the human environment, the conditions which might lead to the registry of this need are almost constantly present. Moreover, human beings are so thoroughly conditioned to the presence of others that they have a strong tendency to project this human factor even into situations where it is not present. We are prone to play to an audience even when there is no audience. Such behavior can be rationalized, when a need for rationalization is felt, in either of two ways. It can be justified on the basis of anticipation, that is, of how other people will react if or when they discover what the individual has done, but it can also be justified in terms of an invisible audience. In the latter case the social milieu is conceived of as including beings who, no matter how they may differ from men in their other attributes, resemble them in their responses to various forms of behavior and in their ability to affect the well-being of the individual. The primitive animist, the believer in observant ancestral spirits and the worshippers of an ever-watchful, all-powerful deity have all chosen this second type of rationalization.

The importance of this social component for the understanding of human behavior can scarcely be overrated. As a result of its presence, behavior patterns which are in process of formation can be rewarded or discouraged not only in terms of whether they achieve their manifest goals but also in terms of the methods by which the individual strives to achieve these goals. The individual who adheres to the socially approved forms of behavior is assured of some reward in the form of favorable response even when his behavior is ineffective in terms of its manifest ends. The attitude of others toward such a failure is summed up in the familiar phrase: "Well, he made a good try." Conversely, the individual who attains his ends by unorthodox and socially disapproved forms of behavior invokes unfavorable responses which rob these ends of much of their value. It is this social component which is primarily responsible for the transmission of complex behavior patterns as wholes from generation to generation. It makes *how* goals are attained nearly as important to the individual as *whether* they are attained. Social pressure keeps the developing behaviors of the individual within the limits set by his society's culture patterns and insures that his emergent habits will be such as to make his behavior predictable in terms of his position within the society. It also insures that these habits will be of a sort congruous with the habits established in other members of the society through the same mechanisms. Without such a social component culture could not be transmitted nor societies perpetuated as functioning wholes.

In summary, the situations which evoke responses from the individual are, with very few exceptions, configurations which include both a particular aggregate of needs and a particular set of conditions under which they have to be satisfied. With this in mind, we may proceed to a consideration of the responses themselves. It is possible to classify these responses in many different ways, depending upon the criteria chosen, and the problem becomes one not of the validity of a particular system of classification but rather of its utility in connection with a particular set of problems. As an aid to the understanding of the interrelations of personality and culture we may divide responses into two main groups:

1. *Emergent responses*
2. *Established responses*

To phrase this in another way, responses may be divided into those which are in process of development and organization and those which have become fully organized and automatized. While the former grade into the latter, the polar positions in the series are clear enough. At the emergent end of the scale we have those behaviors which are evoked by new and unfamiliar situations. Such behaviors are normally tentative and experimental, without consistent organization or patterning. At the established end of the scale we have those behaviors which are evoked by familiar situations. Such behaviors are thoroughly organized and patterned. While the emergent responses always involve some degree of consciousness of the situation and of effort to solve the problem which it presents, established responses are automatic and can be produced without either the registry of the situation or the associated behavior attaining a conscious level.

The responses which any individual is capable of making extend over the full range represented by this scale, but their distribution in the scale is far from uniform. The bulk of such responses always cluster about the established response pole, with an abrupt drop in frequency as one moves toward the emergent response pole. Most of the situations which the individual encounters in the ordinary business of living have become familiar through long repetition and are taken care of by automatized responses, in ordinary parlance, habits. Such habits may involve a good deal of waste motion and often could be made much more effective in terms of their manifest ends. Nevertheless, they are superior to non-habitual responses in terms of the conservation of the individual's nervous energy and diminution of emotional strain. It is easier to live by habit than by conscious intent, and most of us do live by habit most of the time. The discomforts produced by the necessity of developing a large number of new behaviors to meet new situations are abundantly illustrated by the plight of the current group of European refugees. These individuals have been deprived of their familiar milieus and find most of their habits no longer effective. That this results in serious personality derangements in a large number of cases is obvious to anyone who has had to deal with such refugees. Under normal conditions the individual is rarely called upon to meet new situations, and when such situations do arise they present themselves only a few at a time. The fact that we can carry on most of our activities at the habitual level serves to conserve energy and to provide the surplus vigor required to develop new forms of behavior as the need for them arises.

The position of a particular behavioral response in the scale extending from newly emergent to fully established will correspond in general to its position in a developmental sequence by which experimental, more or less conscious responses are transformed into habits. There must always be a first occasion on which a particular situation registers with the individual and a first attempt to meet it. As the situation is repeated, the behavioral responses to it become increasingly organized and are produced with less and less conscious effort. Finally these responses emerge as a single integrated pattern of behavior which is automatically set in train by the registry of the situation. The organized aggregate of habits which have been established in the individual constitute the bulk of his personality and give it form, structure and continuity. In fact we may picture the personality as consisting of an organized, relatively persistent core of habits surrounded by a fluid zone of behavioral responses which are in process of reduction to habitual terms. It follows that the processes involved in the development of new behaviors derive their main functional significance from the contribution which they are able to make to the establishment of new and effective habits. We are prone to think of the intellectual processes as the highest manifestations of individual psychology. Certainly they represent the culmination of the trends discernible in the evolution of psychological potentialities through animals to man. However, we must admit that in most cases their operation is merely a preliminary to habit formation. They assist in and expedite the development of overt behavioral responses, but these responses become of maximum utility only after they have been reduced to automatic, habitual terms.

Since the development of every habit begins with an attempt to meet a new situation, the processes involved in this attempt are of great importance for the understanding of personality formation. It is obvious that processes of various sorts may be invoked, but the relative importance of these various approaches for the development of human behavior is not always recognized. There seems to be a strong tendency on the part of many writers on the subject to accord first place to the intellectual processes and second to those of trial and error. Actually, the *initial* response of any individual who has to develop a new pattern of behavior to meet a new situation usually depends more on *imitation* than on either of these. *Imitation* may be taken to mean copying the behavior of others irrespective of whether the imitator has become acquainted with this behavior through direct observation, through being told about it or, in the more advanced societies, through reading about it. The only conditions under which the imitative technique cannot be applied are (*a*) when the situation is novel for the society as well as the individual and (*b*) when the individual has had no opportunity to learn what other people do in response to the particular situation.

In the normal course of events neither of the above conditions is likely to arise. While every situation which can confront the individual is, at one point, novel for him, very few situations can arise which will be novel for his society as well. As a member of this society he has access to a store of developed behavior patterns which are adequate to meet almost any eventuality. Even situations of extreme rarity are remembered together with the behavior appropriate to them. Thus a total eclipse of the sun will rarely occur more than once in the lifetime of any individual, but practically all societies know that there are eclipses and have stereotyped behavior patterns in connection with them. The effectiveness of such patterns is readily demonstrable, since the sun always comes back. Conditions of isolation under which the individual has to meet a new situation without direct aid from other members of the society are much more likely to arise, but even then he is rarely thrown entirely upon his own resources. All societies devote a great deal of time and energy to training their younger members in what they should do under various hypothetical conditions. Children are instructed not only in the behavior which will be adequate in various situations but also in the cues by which these situations are to be recognized. Although such imitative responses lack the speed and certainty which come with repeated experience, they are exceedingly useful to the individual in meeting emergencies. Thus any boy from a hunting tribe who finds himself alone with darkness falling will know how to go about building a shelter and making himself comfortable even if he has never had to do so before. A city dweller who has never been taught how to do this will be much less successful in taking care of himself. In summary, the individual comes to practically all new situations forearmed with a knowledge of the behavior patterns which other members of his society have developed and tested. It is only when such knowledge is lacking that he has to turn to the laborious process of solving problems for himself.

Even in the rare cases when the individual cannot imitate, adults very rarely resort to the techniques of simple trial and error based upon overt behavior and its observed results. This method is poorly adapted to dealing with situations of any complexity. The young child's tendency to use it is soon extinguished by its frequent failures. Conversely, the child's tendency to imitate is so consistently rewarded that it soon becomes an automatic response evoked by any novel situation. Adults may revert to simple trial and error now and then, but they usually do so only under conditions of emotional stress, as in moments of rage or panic. Thus even the most intelligent adult may turn to it at some stage in a struggle with a refractory suitcase. However, such lapses are temporary. In the absence of patterns to be imitated, the normal adult technique for solving new problems is to appraise the situation in the light of past experience and to devise what one anticipates will be an adequate response before initiating overt behavior. In colloquial terms, we think first and then act. The mechanisms and processes involved in thinking are complex and poorly understood, and we need not attempt to discuss them here. As they relate to the development of new behavior they apparently involve anticipation of the results of various acts and the inhibition of those which will be ineffective. This process has been termed "symbolic trial and error." While such a definition of thinking probably errs on the side of oversimplification, it expresses the functional aspects of the process fairly well. Thinking is certainly a substitute for overt trial and error, and one which performs the same functions with a lesser expenditure of time and energy.

Intellectual processes operate mainly at the conscious level and involve the manipulation of the conscious residues of experience which we term knowledge. The present connotations of this term are so wide that any attempt to discuss the nature of knowledge would carry us out of the area of psychology and anthropology into that of philosophy. However, the individual's conscious residue of experience includes two sorts of elements which can be distinguished on the basis of their functions relative to the development of new behavior patterns. Every individual is familiar with a series of behavior patterns which have been developed by others. He also has a store of more or less unrelated items of information which we may term facts. His knowledge of how to go about building a shelter would be an example of the first, his knowledge that water runs down hill an example of the second. Knowledge of the first type functions as the basis of imitative behavior, and its employment involves the use of memory rather than thought. Knowledge of the second type can be related to behavior only through an intermediate process of organization and correlation by which the relation of certain facts to the probable outcome of certain forms of behavior is foreseen. Although knowledge of particular behavior patterns and their results may be employed in such correlations, that is, may function as factual knowledge, factual knowledge cannot serve as a basis for imitative behavior. Thus while both knowledge of how a shelter can be built and that water runs down hill may influence the development of a new behavior pattern, only the first of these can be used as a basis for imitative behavior.

The individual acquires his fund of knowledge not only as a result of his direct observation and experience, but also through instruction. This introduces a factor which may have curious consequences. That part of knowledge which relates to the behavior patterns of other members within a society is usually a close approximation of reality. On the other hand, items of factual knowledge which have become thoroughly verbalized and which are regularly transmitted within a society acquire a sort of independent existence. They must be regarded as constituting culture patterns in their own right. In many cases this sort of patterning is carried to the point where the culturally established facts not only cease to approximate reality but even become largely immune to the checks provided by first-hand observation and experience. All societies include in their store of transmitted knowledge numerous items which are demonstrably untrue. This is especially the case with respect to knowledge of specific past events. No society ever taught its younger generations the truth about its own history. However, it also applies to many cases in which transmitted knowledge might be susceptible to direct checking by current observation. Thus the knowledge that objects of different weights fall at different speeds was transmitted in western society from the time of Aristotle to that of Galileo. It was only with the development of an all-pervading scepticism and of experimental approaches to the study of natural phenomena that it was consciously subjected to observational tests and became knowledge no longer.

Whether true or false, facts provide the thinking processes with the tools necessary to their operation. Everyone reasons from certain premises, that is, unquestioned items of knowledge, and the nature of these premises is reflected in the conclusions. As far as we can ascertain, the intellectual processes themselves are the same for all normal human beings in all times and places. At least individuals who begin with the same premises always seem to arrive at the same conclusions. It is the universal experience of anthropologists that when they have lived with any "primitive" society long enough to know its premises, they have no difficulty in "thinking native." The seeming illogical conclusions arrived at by members of non-European groups have given rise to numerous treatises on the peculiar qualities of the "primitive" mind, but it is significant that none of these treatises have been written by persons who had an intimate, first-hand knowledge of "primitives." Such conclusions indicate differences in the factual knowledge with which members of different societies operate, not in their mental processes. A tribe which tries to stop a typhoid epidemic by organizing large-scale witch hunts operates logically in terms of the culturally established fact that witches are responsible for disease. When we try to achieve the same end by inoculation and boiling drinking water, we also are acting logically on the basis of our culturally established knowledge that disease is caused by bacteria. Most members of our society have never seen a germ, but they have been taught that germs exist and accept their existence without further proof. Our own not very remote ancestors would have found the witch hunt more logical than the inoculations.

Although the individual's first response to a new situation may be developed primarily through imitation, through logical processes or through trial and error, there are few cases which involve only one of these processes. Even when a particular pattern of behavior has been witnessed repeatedly, the individual who tries to imitate it for the first time finds himself uncertain about some parts of the procedure. If he has only been told about it his uncertainties are multiplied. Such uncertainties constitute a series of minor problems which have to be solved by thought or by trial and error. The way in which these various processes may function together toward the development of a new behavior pattern will be appreciated by anyone who can remember and analyse his first attempt to fix some household electrical appliance. Even the manuals designed to aid in such initial efforts always leave a surprising number of questions unanswered.

The individual's initial attempts to meet new situations are also influenced by what we may call his generalized habitual responses. The nature of these responses will be discussed later in this chapter. As has already been pointed out, every situation is a configuration involving numerous elements. Even when a particular situation configuration is new to the individual, certain of its component elements may be familiar to him in other contexts. On the basis of such similarities he will, often unconsciously, tend to transfer various items of behavior from his established patterns of response to the emergent pattern associated with the new situation. Thus everyone is familiar with a series of situations which involve dealing with someone in authority. Although each of these situations will have its own pattern of automatized response, all these patterns will have certain elements in common. These common elements will include particular attitudes toward authority per se and also certain acts symbolizing the individual's recognition of authority and willingness to submit to it. When a new situation involving the familiar authority factor arises, the elements common to the individual's automatized responses are almost certain to be included in even his first attempts to meet the new situation.

The reduction of emergent responses to automatized ones seems to follow the same course irrespective of the exact methods by which the first successful response was developed. As the situation and response are repeated, the response undergoes modifications which add to its effectiveness in achieving its manifest ends and also serve to adjust it to the particular qualities of the individual. Since much of the behavior involved in the response remains conscious throughout most of the adjustment period, it is subject to deliberate, purposeful modification. Any or all of the processes involved in the development of initial responses may also be involved in their subsequent adjustment. Various items within the emergent response pattern may be modified or replaced as a result of imitation or of trial and error, while the rôle of the intellectual processes in adjustment is, apparently, more important than their rôle in the development of initial responses. Individuals tend to imitate the culture patterns of their society when confronted by a new situation, then to take thought as the situation is repeated and to try to adjust these patterns to their individual needs. Culture patterns come to the individual like suits of ready-made clothes. They represent an approximation of his requirements, but they do not really fit him until they have been taken in in one place and let out in another. Just as with the suit, the patterns within a real culture set ultimate limits to the modifications which may be made, but these limits are usually wide enough to take care of all but the markedly abnormal.

Just what happens to responses during this period of reworking and adjustment is still imperfectly understood and would seem to offer a fertile field for research. Adjustments in terms of increased efficiency with respect to the manifest goals of the response are, it seems, rarely carried through to their ultimate possibilities. At least there is plenty of evidence in the field of overt behavior that acts which do not contribute directly to the attainment of such goals are not automatically eliminated during the adjustment period. This has been brought out repeatedly in studies of the movements employed in various occupations. These can nearly always be simplified and abbreviated, with a resulting gain in efficiency. It seems that when acts which are not actually deleterious become associated with a response, they are likely to become integrated into the response configuration and to be carried along by sheer inertia.

The modifications directed toward the adjustment of response to the particular qualities of the individual seem to be more far-reaching. Such adjustments must take into account physiologically determined factors such as strength, acuity and speed of perception, capacities for muscular coördination, and so forth. They also must, and do, take into account the whole complex of the individual's previously established responses. In other words, the new response must be made congruous with the preëxisting personality configuration, so that it can be incorporated into it without serious conflicts or derangements. Preëxisting automatized responses operate as factors in the shaping of new responses. Even at the level of simple overt behavior there seems to be a strong tendency to incorporate into developing responses whole configurations of movements which have been developed in connection with earlier responses. Thus it is an observed fact that in the technologies of the simpler cultures certain series of movements tend to be employed in several different sorts of manufacture. This may hold even when the materials employed are markedly different in their qualities and potentialities for manipulation. Thus a group which has been accustomed to making coiled basketry usually will, when it turns to pottery making, employ a coiling technique.

In the case of more complex and generalized responses there also seems to be a strong tendency for the individual to adjust his initial response to any situation in terms of his established attitudes. He will also modify and adjust it in terms of the responses, either real or anticipated, which his behavior evokes from others. In the course of its development and transfer to the automatized category, each response will be modified in the direction of producing the minimum of emotional conflict within the individual and the maximum of favorable response from other members of his society. Since there are few cases in which both these ends can be achieved completely and simultaneously, the result is usually a compromise. Moreover, this compromise normally will be weighted in one direction or the other, the direction of weighting being determined by whether the individual finds inner peace or social approval the more valuable. In order to be successful every response must provide some measure of both, but the proportions of each which will satisfy an extrovert will be unsatisfactory to an introvert and vice versa.

In the development of a new habit the processes of modification, of integration into the preëxisting personality configuration and of increasing automatization apparently go on simultaneously. The end product is an automatic response adjusted both to the achievement of its manifest ends and to the other automatic responses of the individual. The whole configuration of such responses takes care of nearly the whole business of living, which can thus be carried on, for the most part, without serious emotional conflicts or involvements and without the exercise of the intellectual faculties. The organization and patterning of this personality configuration is so complex and our techniques for analysing configurations in these terms so rudimentary that it seems safer not to attempt to deal with these aspects of the personality. It does seem possible, however, to analyse the content of established personality configurations in terms of the various sorts of automatized responses which they include.

In seeking for some criterion by which the individual's automatized responses may be differentiated, the factor most important in connection with the relations between personality and culture seems to be that of the *specificity of responses.* In other words, we may take as our starting point the degree to which a particular response is linked with a particular situation to the exclusion of other situations. To understand the nature of this relationship we must remember that every complete response and every situation which evokes such a response is a configuration composed of numerous elements. In habitual reactions of the most specific sort a certain situation as a whole evokes a certain response as a whole, this response being adequate to meet all the conditions imposed by the situation. However, there are also automatized, that is, habitual, responses of a more limited scope. These are evoked by certain elements within situation configurations rather than by such configurations as wholes. A response of this order may be set in train by any situation which includes the elements with which it is linked. It can even be evoked by a situation which is new as a whole if the presence of these elements within the situation configuration is perceived. Thus an anxiety response can be evoked by any one of a great number of situation configurations, all of which have in common the element of threat to the individual. Responses of this type are too generalized to be effective in themselves. They are, from the functional point of view, partial responses which operate primarily as elements in various specific response configurations. However, they play an important rôle in the shaping of the more specific responses into which they are ultimately incorporated. Thus an initial anxiety response will influence the various forms of overt behavior evoked by a particular situation and through this the final form of the specific response to this situation.

In summary, a specific response is one which is evoked by only one or at most a very small number of situations and which is, in itself, effective with respect to these situations. A generalized response is one which may be evoked by a number of different situations which have particular factors in common but which is not, in itself, effective with respect to these situations. On the basis of this distinction, the automatized responses of the individual may be arranged in a series which has at one end those which are exceedingly specific and at the other those which are so generalized that they color wide areas of the individual's behavior. It must be emphasized that this scale is intended simply as a descriptive device. The position of the various responses within it does not correspond to any sort of development sequence.

The most specific type of response would be a pattern of behavior closely adjusted to the conditions imposed by a particular situation and evoked by this situation and no other. Actually, it is difficult to find examples of this type and those which can be cited usually involve very simple behavior. Perhaps the repetitive movements employed in paddling a canoe when someone else is doing the steering would be a case in point for our society. Even this would not hold for certain other societies in which the same overt behavior was linked with other situations, as taking part in a canoe dance. Habitual responses in which the overt behavior is thoroughly patterned but in which it can be evoked by any one of a small series of situations are much commoner. Thus the behavior involved in shaving or taking a shower is, for most American males, automatized and stereotyped even to the musical accompaniments, but it can be evoked by various situations. Either getting up and starting the working day or the need for making oneself presentable for a dinner date will serve to set this response configuration in train.

It is a matter of common experience that most specific responses which have become thoroughly established seem to be almost devoid of emotional content. This holds even when the situations which evoke them elicited strong emotional responses at first. Thus many persons have experienced a strong fear reaction the first time they had to speak in public, but have seen this reaction diminish and disappear as the experience was repeated. There seems to be no generally accepted explanation for this, and the whole field of emotional phenomena is so poorly explored that I hesitate to advance one. However, it is an established fact that most emotional states are accompanied by physiological changes and that the sensations by which the individual recognizes these states are linked with the changes. In the case of active emotions such as fear, the physiological reactions serve to mobilize the organism's reserves of energy and to prepare the individual for heightened activity. As any situation is repeated and an effective response to it developed and reduced to automatic terms, the need for energy mobilization diminishes. An improved evaluation of the situation, that is, a realization that it is less difficult or threatening than at first supposed, must also operate to diminish energy mobilization. With these two factors operating simultaneously the physiological response may diminish until it reaches the point where it no longer registers in terms of sensation, that is, where no emotion is felt. This explanation would seem to be adequate to account for the disappearance of those emotions which are associated with threats to the individual. It is less adequate for situations which initially evoke emotions of pleasure, although in these also the emotional response often seems to be diminished with repetition.

As we proceed from specific responses to those which are increasingly generalized there appears to be a progressive diminution in the extent and elaboration of the overt behavior involved. A generalized response is one which is evoked by several situations or, more accurately, by some factor which is common to a series of situations. Such a generalized response is rarely adequate, in itself, to meet all the situations included in this series. It emerges as a part of the individual's initial unorganized responses to new situations and functions as a component in the *specific* response configurations which he develops through repetition. As a rule, the simpler the overt behavior involved in any generalized response, the greater the number of specific responses into which it can be integrated. Thus a very simple pattern of muscular movements can be incorporated into a much greater number of habitual technological responses than can a lengthy and complicated one.

Actually, many of the individual's most generalized responses involve a very small element of organized, automatic overt behavior. As we approach this end of our scale we find ourselves more and more involved with covert responses whose overt manifestations may assume many different forms. In other words, we pass from the field of habits, in the popular usage of the term, into that of *values* and *attitudes*. These terms are borrowed from the social sciences. Although there seems to be considerable confusion in their usage in that field, they have a commonly accepted core of meaning which makes them better adapted to our purposes than new and unfamiliar terms would be. For our present purposes, a *value* may be defined as any element, common to a series of situations, which is capable of evoking a covert response in the individual. An *attitude* may be defined as the covert response evoked by such an element. The content of such responses seems to be largely emotional but may include other types of response such as anticipations. The value and attitude together form a stimulus-response configuration which we will refer to as a *value-attitude system*. Once established in the individual, such systems operate automatically and, for the most part, below the level of consciousness. A single system of this sort may underlie several different patterns of overt behavior, providing motivations for all of them. Thus the individual's value-attitude system relative to cruelty may lead him to withdraw in one situation or to interfere in another.

The functional importance of value-attitude systems derives primarily from their emotional content. Behavior which is not in accord with the individual's system elicits responses of fear, anger or, at the very least, disapproval. This holds equally whether the behavior is his own or that of others. Thus an individual who performs an act contrary to one of his own established value-attitude systems will experience considerable emotional disturbance both before and after. In most cases he will have such a reaction even though he knows that the act will not entail punishment. This disturbance will diminish with repetitions of the act, but will reappear with each new situation involving the particular system. Similarly, other people's acts which are contrary to one of these systems will elicit emotional responses even when they do not threaten the individual in any way. This projective aspect of value-attitude systems will be familiar to anyone who has had to adjust himself to life in an alien society and culture. Even when the members of such a society are completely friendly and coöperative, merely observing certain of their behavior patterns is likely to make the outsider exceedingly uncomfortable. Thus most Americans in Latin countries react strongly to certain local customs which are not in agreement with our values of modesty and sanitation. They also find it hard to adjust to the casual and unconscious cruelty to animals which is a feature of many cultures and are, at first, deeply affected by such acts as the plucking of fowls alive.

Value-attitude systems may vary considerably in their specificity. The test used to establish the position of responses in the scale which we have set up is a purely objective one. The smaller the number of situations which evoke a particular response, the more specific we consider it. On this basis, certain attitude responses are more specific than many of the simpler overt behavioral responses. However, certain attitudes achieve a degree of generalization rarely if ever equaled by overt responses. Thus there are certain attitudes which are evoked by so many situations that they influence the bulk of the individual's behavior. It is on the basis of such highly generalized attitudes that we characterize certain individuals as optimistic or pessimistic, trusting or suspicious, introvert or extrovert. In such cases the mere registry of a new situation which must be met, irrespective of its particular qualities, is enough to set in train emotional responses and anticipations of a characteristic sort. Such generalized attitudes underlie more specific value-attitude systems and influence their development in very much the way that the latter underlie and influence habitual patterns of overt behavior. Thus an insecure individual may come to regard all situations which involve dealing with superiors as threatening and to react to such situations automatically in terms of fear and hostility.

It is significant that many of the value-attitude systems which are shared and transmitted by the members of a society are important to the well-being of the society rather than to that of the individual. Thus under ordinary circumstances the coward has a better chance of survival than the brave man, yet all societies try to establish in their members value-attitude systems which will promote brave behavior. Since courage is necessary for the successful defense of the group, such systems contribute to the survival of the society at the expense of its individual members. The individual acquires such desirable but personally disadvantageous value-attitude systems as a result of the social rewards which come with their assumption and incorporation into specific patterns of overt response. Although courageous behavior may cost a man his life in the long run, meanwhile it brings him respect and admiration. The goal of eliciting favorable response from others stands side by side with every one of the individual's more immediate and specific goals, and no pattern of behavior can be completely successful and rewarding unless it serves to achieve both.

Up to this point our discussion has dealt with the development, nature and operation of automatized behavioral responses. It remains to deal with one other aspect of the problem: their extinction. The personality is not only a continuum but also a continuum in a constant state of change. The process of developing and integrating new responses and extinguishing old ones goes on throughout the lifetime of the individual. Without such flexibility it would be impossible for him to survive in a world in which not only the external environment but also his own potentialities are in a constant state of flux. However, there seems to be a fairly close correlation between the ease with which a particular response can be extinguished and its position in the scale of specificity. In general, the more specific a response the easier it is to extinguish it. The reason for this is fairly obvious. Laboratory experiments have shown that habits are extinguished either when they fail to achieve the desired ends or when they expose the individual to too much punishment. Owing to environmental or other changes, a response which is linked with a single situation or with a very small number of situations, can easily become subject to the conditions which will lead to extinction. More generalized responses, on the other hand, are likely to be rewarded in connection with some situations even when they are unrewarded or punished in connection with others. It is a common experience that while specific patterns of overt behavior are fairly easy to extinguish, value-attitude systems are extremely hard to extinguish. Such systems tend to survive even when their overt expressions have been inhibited in many situations and to reassert themselves with almost undiminished vigor when new situations involving the particular value factor arise.

There also appears to be some correlation between the position of a response in the scale of specificity and the ease with which it can be established at any given point in the life cycle. The correlations are less clear in this case than in that of extinction, and the whole matter merits further investigation. In general, it seems fairly easy to establish specific responses, especially those which primarily involve overt behavior, at any point in the life cycle. It is commonly believed that even these can be established more readily in childhood than in later life but I am not sure that this has been proved. On the other hand, generalized responses of the value-attitude type seem to be easy to establish in childhood but exceedingly difficult to establish in adult life. The reasons for this are not clear but one or two possible explanations may be hazarded. It has already been pointed out that value-attitude systems underlie and function as elements in whole series of more specific situation responses. It seems possible that, in the adult, the assumption of a new value-attitude system necessarily involves so many readjustments in his established specific responses that it is more trouble than it is worth. In psychological parlance, the punishment resulting from such a response outweighs its possible rewards. The same conditions would be operative in connection with the extinction of adult value-attitude systems, the complex integration of such systems into a large series of specific responses making their elimination in itself a source of discomfort. There is also a possibility, however, that the observed tendency for exceedingly generalized attitudes to become established in early childhood is linked with some inability on the part of the small child to differentiate between related situations. With this would be associated an inability to develop clearly defined configurations of specific behavior with regard to each of the situations in a related series. Thus the equation of a number of situations on the basis of a common factor, say the presence of an adult, and the development of a single generalized response to all of them might, if the response was rewarded, result in the establishment of a particular attitude. This attitude might, in turn, be reflected in later and more specific patterns of response as these were developed. However, in the present state of our knowledge such explanations are pure conjecture.

The formulations of personality formation and content which have just been presented are simply attempts to arrange a collection of facts and bring them into some sort of intelligible order. Any number of other arrangements of the same facts are possible. The value of any system of this sort lies entirely in its utility. There is no yardstick of absolute truth against which various systems can be measured, and the system which may be most useful in connection with one set of problems may be almost useless in connection with another. Most of the disputes which enliven the field of psychology seem to originate either in the natural tendency of systematizers to identify with the systems they have set up or in the inability of investigators to recognize familiar phenomena when described in unfamiliar terms. These difficulties are increased by differences in the immediate interests of various schools of psychology. The Behaviorists, in keeping with their devotion to techniques of controlled experiment, have focused their attention on the overt behavioral aspects of response. Depth Psychologists, on the other hand, have focused theirs on the covert aspects. This is readily understandable in view of the nature of the material with which they have had to deal. Depth psychology began as a by-product of psychotherapy, and the practitioner has to take his patients as he finds them.

In the formulations which I have just presented it is assumed that every response is a configuration which includes both overt and covert elements. At the same time it has been emphasized that the proportion of elements of each of these orders relative to the total content of the response configuration may vary greatly. In spite of certain exceptions, it may be laid down as a rule that the more specific a response, the greater the proportion of overt relative to covert elements. Conversely, the more generalized a response, the greater the proportion of covert elements relative to overt ones. Thus toward one end of the scale of specificity we have habits of the sort with which the Behaviorists have been primarily concerned. Toward the other end of the scale we have the attitudes with which Depth Psychologists have been primarily concerned. In general, the concept of depth employed by these psychologists can be directly equated with that of generalization employed in the present formulation. No attempt has been made to isolate particular groups of deep, or generalized responses in terms of their special functions. This means that such concepts as that of the Id, the Ego and the Superego cannot be equated with the present formulation. The validity of such functional discriminations is not questioned, but they do not appear necessary for our present purposes. It may be added that in terms of my formulation a neurosis would be classed as a generalized response, one of the individual's value-attitude systems. It would differ from the individual's other value-attitude systems mainly in the fact that it was *individual*, that is, not shared by most members of the particular society. Value-attitude systems which are largely shared are normally adjusted to the society's culturally established patterns of overt behavior. The individual can thus express them in his own behavior without involving himself in difficulties or conflicts. Individual value-attitude systems, on the other hand, lead those who have them to develop specific overt behavioral responses which are not adjusted to the cultural and social milieu within which such persons have to operate. This lack of judgment gives rise to internal conflicts and frustrations and also elicits unfavorable response from others.

I feel that the correlation of the formulations which I have just presented with the concept of the individual's Projective System, as developed by Dr. A. Kardiner,[1] deserves special attention. This is particularly the case since I owe much of my interest in, and knowledge of, personality psychology to my association with Dr. Kardiner in various researches on the interrelations of personality and culture. The individual's projective system may, I believe, be taken to correspond to the whole series of highly generalized responses, predominantly covert in their content,

[1] A. Kardiner, *Psychological Frontiers of Society* (New York, Columbia University Press, 1944).

which are established in the individual as a result of his experiences. These responses function both as a component in the individual's appraisal of new situations as they arise and in his development of more specific and predominantly overt responses to such situations. The generalized responses which constitute the projective system seem to be established, for the most part, during the individual's early formative period. Since the experience responsible for them is largely derived from contact with the culturally patterned behavior of other individuals, the norms for projective systems will tend to differ in different societies. This fact has important implications for the understanding of a wide range of social and cultural phenomena as these appear in time as well as space.

The formulations which I have presented are intended primarily as an aid to the correlation of cultural and psychological phenomena. Since the next chapter will be devoted to a discussion of the rôle of culture in personality formation, we may limit ourselves for the present to static correlations. Cultures, like personalities, are continuums in a constant state of change and as such have their own processes of growth, of establishment of new response patterns, and of elimination of old ones. These processes parallel those which go on within the personality and are dependent, in the last analysis, upon the ability of a society's members to develop new forms of behavior, to learn and to forget. However, cultural processes normally operate over time spans much longer than those comprised within the life cycle of any one member of a society. They also differ from the processes involved in the formation of the individual personality in certain important respects. Thus the origination of new forms of behavioral response seems to be a function not of the society as a whole but of some one, or at the most a few, of the individuals who compose the society. In colloquial parlance, there can be no invention without an inventor. Moreover, the final stabilization and integration of a new pattern of response into the society's culture is not always a matter of the progressive modification and adjustment of a single response pattern. It is much more likely to be preceded by a period during which several relatively well-organized and -adjusted patterns of response to the particular situation compete for social acceptance.

It is significant that cultural processes, and indeed culture as a whole, seem to have little effect upon the *processes* involved in the development and operation of the personality. The personality processes derive from the qualities which are inherent in the human organism. They represent the individual's psychological potentialities in action. Culture, through the experience which the individual derives from his contact with it, determines a part of the materials with which the personality processes operate. Examples of this have already been given in our discussion of the rôle of the intellectual processes in the development of new response patterns. It was shown in this discussion how culturally determined materials, in this case knowledge, influence the results of the operation of personality processes. However, such materials derive from the content of culture, not from its processes per se. Culture processes parallel personality processes at many points, but it is questionable whether any exact correlations between the two can be established.

When we turn to a comparison of culture content and personality content, the correlations are much more obvious. In both its qualities and its relations to the larger configuration of which it forms a part, the fully developed, automatized response of the individual is almost the exact equivalent of a real culture pattern.[1] For the sake of brevity, individual responses of this automatized type will henceforth be referred to as habits. Both the habit and the culture pattern represent a limited range of behavioral responses which are evoked by a limited series of situations. The evoking situations are equated on the basis of their common elements and their individual variations are not linked with specific variations in the responses within the corresponding response series. In both the habit and the culture pattern a mode for the range of responses can be established by statistical methods. It has been pointed out in a previous chapter that an individual habit mode usually does not correspond exactly with the mode of the culture pattern with which this habit is to be equated. Both the habit and the real culture pattern are always adjusted to the other elements in the configuration of which they form a part. With both the development of such adjustments is a constant accompaniment of the processes of stabilization and integration.

Although none of the current formulations of culture content have attempted to range culture patterns in a series based on degrees of specificity, this criterion

[1] For definition of a real culture pattern see p. 45.

can be applied to them quite as readily as to habits. Culture patterns range from those which provide adequate response to a single situation through value-attitude systems to responses of a highly generalized type. It may be remembered that in a previous chapter I drew a distinction between the overt and covert aspects of culture. The main value of such a distinction is that it differentiates clearly between those elements of culture whose presence can be ascertained by direct observation and those whose presence can only be deduced. Actually, every culture pattern includes both overt and covert elements which have been organized into a functional whole. One is tempted to project the correlation between specificity and subjective content which is present in the case of habits into the field of culture patterns. It would be a great satisfaction to the tidy-minded if it could be shown that specific culture patterns include, as a rule, a low proportion of covert elements and highly generalized culture patterns a high one. It seems that some tendency in this direction is recognizable. Certainly the covert content of a cultural value-attitude system is, in most cases, proportionally much higher than that of a cultural pattern for making a basket. However, one could cite numerous exceptions to such a rule, and the correlation is certainly much less close for culture patterns than for habits. It might be added that with respect to emotional affect, not to be confused with covert culture, there seems to be no correlation between degree of affect and specificity of culture pattern. Thus most societies have very specific patterns for dealing with such offences as murder or incest, yet the emotional reactions of members of the group to these offences are of the most vigorous sort. It seems probable that a frequency factor is operative here. Rare events even when linked with highly specific culture patterns seem to have a greater capacity for evoking emotional response than do common ones.

Most of the correlations which have just been shown to exist between personality content and culture content are of only academic interest. The really significant correlations are those which reflect the influence of culture upon the development of the personality. We will attempt to deal with these in the next, and last, chapter.

5

The Rôle of Culture in Personality Formation

ONE of the most important scientific developments of modern times has been the recognition of culture. It has been said that the last thing which a dweller in the deep sea would be likely to discover would be water. He would become conscious of its existence only if some accident brought him to the surface and introduced him to air. Man, throughout most of his history, has been only vaguely conscious of the existence of culture and has owed even this consciousness to contrasts between the customs of his own society and those of some other with which he happened to be brought into contact. The ability to see the culture of one's own society as a whole, to evaluate its patterns and appreciate their implications, calls for a degree of objectivity which is rarely if ever achieved. It is no accident that the modern scientist's understanding of culture has been derived so largely from the study of non-European cultures where observation could be aided by contrast. Those who know no culture other than their own cannot know their own. Until very recent times even psychologists have failed to appreciate that all human beings, themselves included, develop and function in an environment which is, for the most part, culturally determined. As long as they limited their investigations to individuals reared within the frame of a single culture they could not fail to arrive at concepts of human nature which were far from the truth. Even such a master as Freud frequently posited instincts to account for reactions which we now see as directly referable to cultural conditioning. With the store of knowledge of other societies and cultures which is now available, it is possible to approach the study of personality with fewer preconceptions and to reach a closer approximation of the truth.

It must be admitted at once that the observation and recording of data on personality in non-European societies is still fraught with great difficulty. It is hard enough to get reliable material in our own. The development of accurate, objective techniques for personality study is still in its infancy. Such appliances as the Rorschach tests and Murray's thematic aperception tests have proved their value, but those who have worked with them would be the first to recognize their limitations. In the present state of our knowledge we still have to rely very largely upon informal observations and upon the subjective judgments of the observer. To complicate matters still further, most, although by no means all, of the information which we have on personality in non-European societies has been collected by anthropologists who had only a nodding acquaintance with psychology. Such observers, among whom I include myself at the time that I did most of my ethnological field work, are seriously handicapped by their ignorance of what to look for and what should be recorded. Moreover, there is a lamentable lack of comparative material on the various non-European societies which have been studied. The rapidity with which primitive societies have been acculturated or extinguished during the last hundred years has led to the development of a particular pattern of anthropological investigation. Since there were always far more societies available for study than there were anthropologists to study them and since most of these societies had to be investigated immediately or not at all, each investigator sought a new and unknown group. As a result, most of the information which we have has been collected by one investigator per society. The disadvantages of this are obvious in any case, but especially so in connection with personality studies. In a field where so much depends upon the subjective judgment of the observer and upon the particular members of the society with whom he was able to establish intimate contacts, the personality of the observer becomes a factor in every record. It is to be hoped that with the increasing number of anthropologists and the dwindling number of unstudied societies this pattern of exclusiveness will be broken down and that personality studies will benefit accordingly.

In spite of this frank recognition of difficulties and limitations which only time can remove, certain facts seem to be well established. All anthropologists who have come to know the members of non-European societies intimately are in substantial agreement on certain points. These are: (1) Personality norms differ in different societies. (2) The members of any society will always show considerable individual variation in personality. (3) Much of the same range of variation and much the same personality types are to be found in all societies. Although anthropologists base these conclusions on informal observations, they seem to be substantiated by the results of certain objective tests. Thus Rorschach series from different societies reveal different norms for such series as wholes. They also reveal a wide range of individual variation within each series and much overlapping between series. Even without this evidence, the consensus of opinion on the part of those who should be in a position to know cannot be dismissed lightly. In the absence of more complete and accurate information it seems justifiable to accept these conclusions as facts and to take them as the starting point for our investigation of the rôle of culture in personality formation.

That the norms for personality differ in different societies will scarcely be doubted by anyone who has had experience of societies other than his own. In fact the average individual tends to exaggerate rather than minimize such differences. The only question likely to be raised in this connection is whether a given society should be thought of as having a single personality norm or as having a series of different personality norms each of which is associated with a particular status group within the society. Any difficulty in reconciling these two points of view will disappear when one sees them in proper perspective. The members of any society will always be found to have a long series of personality elements in common. These elements may be of any degree of specificity, ranging from simple overt responses of the sort involved in "table manners" to highly generalized attitudes. Responses of the latter type may underlie a wide range of more specific responses in the individual. Similarly, value-attitude systems which are shared by the members of a society may be reflected in several different forms of status-linked overt behavior. Thus the men and women within a society may share the same attitudes with respect to feminine modesty or masculine courage, although the behavior linked with these attitudes will necessarily be different for each sex. For the women the common modesty attitudes will be expressed in particular patterns of dress or conduct, for the men in more generalized responses of approval or disapproval for particular costumes or conduct. These common personality elements together form a fairly well-integrated configuration which may be called the *Basic Personality Type* for the society as a whole. The existence of this configuration provides the members of the society with common understandings and values and makes possible the unified emotional response of the society's members to situations in which their common values are involved.

It will also be found that in every society there are additional configurations of responses which are linked with certain socially delimited groups within the society. Thus, in practically all cases, different response configurations are characteristic for men and for women, for adolescents and for adults, and so on. In a stratified society similar differences may be observed between the responses characteristic of individuals from different social levels, as nobles, commoners and slaves. These status-linked response configurations may be termed *Status Personalities*. They are of the utmost importance to the successful functioning of the society, since they make it possible for its members to interact successfully on the basis of status cues alone. Thus even in dealings between complete strangers, simple recognition of the social positions of the two individuals involved makes it possible for each to predict how the other will respond to most situations.

The status personalities recognized by any society are superimposed upon its basic personality type and are thoroughly integrated with the latter. However, they differ from the basic personality type in being heavily weighted on the side of specific overt responses. The weighting is so pronounced that it might even be questioned whether status personalities can be said to include any value-attitude systems distinct from those included in the basic personality. However, I feel that it is legitimate to distinguish between *knowledge* of a particular value-attitude system and *participation* in such a system. A status personality will rarely include any value-attitude system which is unknown to the members of other status groups, although it might come to do so under conditions of extreme intergroup hostility. On the other hand, it may very well include value-attitude systems in which the members of other status groups do not participate. Thus free men may know and allow for the attitudes of slaves without actually sharing them. In any case, it is the specific, overt responses which give status personalities most of their social significance. As long as the individual develops these responses, he can function successfully in the status whether he shares the associated value-attitude systems or not. Informal observation leads us to believe that such cases are fairly numerous in all societies. The specific response patterns of a status personality are presented to the individual in simple, concrete terms which make it easy to learn them. Social pressure toward their assumption is constant, and adherence to them is socially rewarded and deviation from them punished. Even the internal conflicts which may arise during the assumption of a specific response pattern which is at variance with one of the individual's value-attitude systems are not too disturbing. Although they may be vigorous at first, they tend to diminish and finally disappear as the response becomes automatized and unconscious.

Every society has its own basic personality type and its own series of status personalities differing in some respects from those of any other society. Practically all societies tacitly recognize this fact, and many of them have explanations for it. Our own society has, until very recent times, based its explanation on biological factors. Differences in basic personality type have been regarded as due to some linkage between race and personality. Status personality differences have been re-referred to sexual factors, in the case of male and female statuses, or to heredity. The latter explanation is not too familiar to Americans, since it is one of our culture patterns to ignore the existence of status personalities other than those which are sex-linked, but it is an integral part of European culture. Folk tales inherited from the days of a rigidly stratified society bristle with incidents in which the child of noble ancestry reared by low-rank foster parents is immediately recognized by his real relatives on the basis of his noble personality. These biological explanations are a good example of the sort of culturally transmitted "knowledge" discussed in the previous chapter. They have been passed on in our society for many generations, and it is only recently that anyone has had the temerity to subject them to the tests of scientific investigation. Such an investigation really has to deal with three distinct problems: (1) In how far is personality determined by physiological factors? (2) In how far are such physiological determinants hereditary? (3) What is the probability of such hereditary determinants becoming so widely diffused in a society as to affect its basic personality type, or, in stratified societies, its status personalities?

We have already seen that the personality is primarily a configuration of responses which the individual has developed as a result of his experience. This experience, in turn, derives from his interaction with his environment. The innate qualities of the individual will influence strongly the sort of experience which he derives from this interaction. Thus a particular environmental situation may result in one sort of experience for a strong child and a quite different sort for a weak one. Again, there are many situations which will result in one sort of experience for an intelligent child and another sort for a dull one. However, it is also obvious that two children of equal intelligence or strength may derive quite different experience from different situations. If one of them is the brightest member of his family and the other the dullest member of his, their experience and the resulting response configurations will be quite different. In other words, although the innate qualities of the individual influence personality development, the sort of influence which they exert will be largely conditioned by environmental factors. Everything which we now know of the processes of personality formation indicates that we must substitute for the old formula of nature versus nurture, a new formula of nature plus or minus nurture. There seems to be abundant evidence that neither innate abilities nor environment can be regarded as constantly dominant in personality formation. Moreover, it appears that different combinations of the two may produce closely similar results as far as the developed personality is concerned. Thus any combination of innate and environmental factors which places the individual in a secure and dominant position will result in the development of certain basic attitudes; any combination which exposes him to insecurity and a subordinate position will result in the development of others.

It seems safe to conclude that innate, biologically determined factors cannot be used to account for personality configurations as wholes or for the various response patterns included within such configurations. They operate simply as one among several sets of factors responsible for the formation of these. However, the personality configuration consists of more than response patterns. It includes certain features of allover organization which are vaguely referred to as the individual's temperament. The current definitions of this term imply that these features are innate and physiologically determined, but it is still uncertain in how far this is really the case. We do not know, for example, whether such a feature as nervous instability is really innate or a result of environmental influences or, as seems most probable, a product of the interaction of innate and environmental factors. Until this question can be answered it seems safest to leave temperament out of the discussion, while recognizing that such an omission must leave our conclusions incomplete.

In addition to response patterns and "temperamental" factors, every personality configuration includes the ability to carry on various psychological processes. It might be safer to speak of abilities, since there is plenty of evidence that a given individual may differ markedly in his facility with respect to different processes. Thus low intelligence may be linked with extraordinary ability in certain forms of learning and memory. That there are also individual differences with respect to particular abilities no one will question, although these differences seem to be a matter of degree rather than of kind. Thus all individuals are capable of some measure of learning and of thought, but they differ widely in their facility with respect to these processes. While facility can be increased by training and practice, the observed differences seem to be too great to be accounted for on this basis alone. Thus it may be questioned whether any amount of training would enable the average individual to memorize the entire Bible or to equal many of the recorded feats of lightning calculators. We are forced to conclude that there are certain innate factors which set upper limits to the possible development of particular psychological abilities and that these factors vary from one individual to another. We may also assume that such factors have some sort of physiological basis, although we still have no clear idea of what this basis may be.

To sum up, it appears that physiological factors cannot be held accountable for the developed response patterns which compose the bulk of the personality but that they may be responsible, in part, for the individual's psychological abilities. This brings us at once to our second problem: "In how far are such physiological determinants hereditary?" Unfortunately we are unable to solve this problem on the basis of our present knowledge or techniques. There is no way in which we can analyse out the psychological abilities of the individual in their "pure" state. We can only judge them by their overt manifestations, and these are always influenced by past experience. The unsatisfactory results obtained when even the best intelligence tests are applied to groups with different culture backgrounds brings this out clearly. This makes it impossible to establish the innate abilities of individuals in the terms required for a real genetic study. We can never tell in how far the apparent intelligence level of any individual is due to heredity or to opportunity. If we grant that psychological abilities have a physiological basis, it seems highly probable that at least some of the physiological factors involved are affected by heredity. At the same time, such evidence as we have on the occurrence of various levels of psychological ability seems to indicate that these are not inherited directly. Their appearance in individuals of known heredity cannot be predicted in the same simple mathematical terms as that of, say, eye color. In view of the almost infinite series of individual gradations in these abilities, it would be surprising if they were inherited directly. The most probable explanation seems to be that the physiological factors which are responsible for a particular level of ability result from certain highly complex combinations of genes and that in heredity these combinations do not move as units.

Even if this explanation is correct, it does not rule out the possibility that the basic personality type for a society may, in certain cases, be influenced by hereditary factors. The members of any society normally tend to intermarry among themselves. If the society is able to maintain its isolation for a long enough period, all its members will come to have much the same heredity. The length of time required to arrive at this condition will depend both upon the size of the original group from which the society's members are descended and on the homogeneity of this group's ancestry. The larger the original group and the more heterogeneous its origins, the longer the time required to establish a homogeneous heredity in its descendants. When the genes required to produce a particular combination are present in the bulk of a society's members, the chances of the combination appearing among their offspring is greatly increased. There is thus an excellent possibility that a small, long-isolated population may come to include a large proportion of individuals who stand at a particular level of psychological ability. Even in closely inbred societies there is always a considerable range of individual variation, so that the stupidest member of an intelligent group might well

CULTURE AND PERSONALITY FORMATION 137

be duller than the most intelligent member of a stupid one. However, the basic personality type for any society is a matter of averages, and these averages may differ from one society to another as a result of hereditary factors. For the reasons already stated, such hereditary differences in psychological abilities would be especially likely to occur in small "primitive" societies of the sort with which anthropological studies have, for the most part, concerned themselves.

The foregoing discussion of the possibility of hereditary differences in the psychological norms for various societies may seem unnecessarily detailed. However, there is strong disagreement on this point even among anthropologists. One group takes it for granted that there are marked differences in the inherited abilities of most societies, while the other flatly denies the possibility of such differences. Apparently neither group has troubled to examine its position in the light of modern knowledge of genetics. The truth almost certainly lies somewhere between the two extremes. Small, long-isolated societies probably do differ in their inherited psychological potentialities. On the other hand, the members of most large societies, and indeed of all civilized ones, are so heterogeneous in their heredity that any physiological explanation of the observed differences in the personality norms for such societies is quite untenable. The genetic differences between, for example, the French and the Germans are so much smaller than the differences in their personality norms that it is ridiculous to try to account for the latter on a genetic basis. Even the most racialistic Germans have had to introduce the mystic concept of a

Nordic soul capable of incarnation in a Mediterranean or Alpine body to bolster their concepts of racial superiority.

American anthropologists, led by the late Dr. Boas, were among the first to recognize the inadequacy of hereditary physiological factors as an explanation of the differing personality norms for various societies. Unfortunately, in their eagerness to combat doctrines of racial inequality and to emphasize the essential unity of our species they overlooked one important point. The processes of scientific advance, aside from the simple gathering of facts, are primarily processes of substitution. When accumulating knowledge renders one explanation of a particular phenomenon untenable, a new and better explanation has to be developed. It is not enough simply to point out that the previously accepted explanation was wrong. It is a readily observable fact that the personality norms for different societies do differ. Instead of accepting this frankly and attempting to account for it, certain anthropologists have contented themselves with trying to minimize the extent and importance of such differences. They have mustered the evidence to show that the differences which they are willing to admit cannot be due to racial factors, but they have done little to develop any better explanation. The belief that the differences in personality norms for various societies are due to innate hereditary factors is deeply rooted in the popular mind. It cannot be eradicated unless science is prepared to offer a better explanation. To believe that all human groups have the same psychological potentialities without trying to account for their very obvious differ-

CULTURE AND PERSONALITY FORMATION 139

ences in overt behavior and even in value-attitude systems, calls for a degree of faith in scientific authority of which few individuals are capable. Even general statements that the observed differences are due to cultural factors remain unconvincing as long as they are not accompanied by explanations of what these factors may be and how they operate.

Our discussion of the possible rôle of hereditary factors in determining the personality norms for various societies should have made it clear that these factors are quite inadequate to account for many of the observable differences. The only alternative is to assume that such differences are referable to the particular environments within which the members of various societies are reared. As has been pointed out elsewhere, the environmental factors which appear to be most important in connection with personality formation are people and things. The behavior of the members of any society and the forms of most of the objects which they use are largely stereotyped and can be described in terms of culture patterns. When we say that the developing individual's personality is shaped by culture, what we actually mean is that it is shaped by the experience which he derives from his contact with such stereotypes. That it actually is shaped by such contacts to a very large extent will hardly be doubted by anyone familiar with the evidence; however, the literature on the subject seems to have largely ignored one important aspect of the shaping process.

The influences which culture exerts on the developing personality are of two quite different sorts.

On the one hand we have those influences which derive from the culturally patterned behavior of other individuals *toward* the child. These begin to operate from the moment of birth and are of paramount importance during infancy. On the other hand we have those influences which derive from the individual's observation of, or instruction in, the patterns of behavior characteristic of his society. Many of these patterns do not affect him directly, but they provide him with models for the development of his own habitual responses to various situations. These influences are unimportant in early infancy but continue to affect him throughout life. The failure to distinguish between these two types of cultural influence has led to a good deal of confusion.

It must be admitted at once that the two types of influence overlap at certain points. Culturally patterned behavior directed toward the child may serve as a model for the development of some of his own behavior patterns. This factor becomes operative as soon as the child is old enough to observe and remember what other people are doing. When, as an adult, he finds himself confronted by the innumerable problems involved in rearing his own children, he turns to these childhood memories for guidance. Thus in almost any American community we find parents sending their children to Sunday School because they themselves were sent to Sunday School. The fact that, as adults, they greatly prefer golf to church attendance does little to weaken the pattern. However, this aspect of any society's patterns for child-rearing is rather incidental to the influence which such patterns exert upon personality formation. At most it insures that children born into a particular society will be reared in much the same way generation after generation. The real importance of the patterns for early care and child-training lies in their effects upon the deeper levels of the personalities of individuals reared according to them.

It is generally accepted that the first few years of the individual's life are crucial for the establishment of the highly generalized value-attitude systems which form the deeper levels of personality content. The first realization of this fact came from the study of atypical individuals in our own society and the discovery that certain of their peculiarities seemed to be rather consistently linked with certain sorts of atypical childhood experiences. The extension of personality studies to other societies in which both the normal patterns of child-rearing and the normal personality configurations for adults were different from our own only served to emphasize the importance of very early conditioning. Many of the "normal" aspects of European personalities which were accepted at first as due to instinctive factors are now recognized as results of our own particular patterns of child care. Although study of the relations between various societies' techniques for child-rearing and the basic personality types for adults in these societies has barely begun, we have already reached a point where certain correlations seem to be recognizable. Although a listing of all these correlations is impossible in a discussion as brief as the present one, a few examples may serve for illustration.

In societies in which the culture pattern prescribes

absolute obedience from the child to the parent as a prerequisite for rewards of any sort, the normal adult will tend to be a submissive individual, dependent and lacking in initiative. Even though he has largely forgotten the childhood experiences which led to the establishment of these attitudes, his first reaction to any new situation will be to look to someone in authority for support and direction. It is worth noting in this connection that there are many societies in which the patterns of child-rearing are so effective in producing adult personalities of this type that special techniques have been developed for training a few selected individuals for leadership. Thus, among the Tanala of Madagascar, eldest sons are given differential treatment from birth, this treatment being designed to develop initiative and willingness to assume responsibility, while other children are systematically disciplined and repressed. Again, individuals who are reared in very small family groups of our own type have a tendency to focus their emotions and their anticipations of reward or punishment on a few other individuals. In this they are harking back unconsciously to a childhood in which all satisfactions and frustrations derived from their own fathers and mothers. In societies where the child is reared in an extended family environment, with numerous adults about, any one of whom may either reward or punish, the normal personality will tend in the opposite direction. In such societies the average individual is incapable of strong or lasting attachments or hatreds toward particular persons. All personal interactions embody an unconscious attitude of: "Oh well, another will be along presently." It is difficult to conceive of such a society embodying in its culture such patterns as our concepts of romantic love, or of the necessity for finding the one and only partner without whom life will be meaningless.

Such examples could be multiplied indefinitely, but the above will serve to show the sort of correlations which are now emerging from studies of personality and culture. These correlations reflect linkages of a simple and obvious sort, and it is already plain that such one-to-one relationships between cause and effect are in the minority. In most cases we have to deal with complex configurations of child-training patterns which, as a whole, produce complex personality configurations in the adult. Nevertheless, no one who is familiar with the results which have already been obtained can doubt that here lies the key to most of the differences in basic personality type which have hitherto been ascribed to hereditary factors. The "normal" members of different societies owe their varying personality configurations much less to their genes than to their nurseries.

While the culture of any society determines the deeper levels of its members' personalities through the particular techniques of child-rearing to which it subjects them, its influence does not end with this. It goes on to shape the rest of their personalities by providing models for their specific responses as well. This latter process continues throughout life. As the individual matures and then ages, he constantly has to unlearn patterns of response which have ceased to be effective and to learn new ones more appropriate to his current place in the society. At every step in this process, culture serves as a guide. It not only provides him with models for his changing rôles but also insures that these rôles shall be, on the whole, compatible with his deep-seated value-attitude systems. All the patterns within a single culture tend to show a sort of psychological coherence quite aside from their functional interrelations. With rare exceptions, the "normal" individual who adheres to them will not be required to do anything which is incompatible with the deeper levels of his personality structure. Even when one society borrows patterns of behavior from another, these patterns will usually be modified and reworked until they become congruous with the basic personality type of the borrowers. Culture may compel the atypical individual to adhere to forms of behavior which are repugnant to him, but when such behavior is repugnant to the bulk of a society's members, it is culture which has to give way.

Turning to the other side of the picture, the acquisition of new behavior patterns which are congruous with the individual's generalized value-attitude systems tends to reinforce these systems and to establish them more firmly as time passes. The individual who spends his life in any society with a fairly stable culture finds his personality becoming more firmly integrated as he grows older. His adolescent doubts and questionings with respect to the attitudes implicit in his culture disappear as he reaffirms them in his adherence to the overt behavior which his culture prescribes. In time he emerges as a pillar of society, unable to understand how anyone can entertain such doubts. While this process may not make for progress, it certainly makes for individual contentment. The state of such a person is infinitely happier than that of one who finds himself compelled to adhere to patterns of overt behavior which are not congruous with the value-attitude systems established by his earliest experiences. The result of such incongruities can be seen in many individuals who have had to adapt to rapidly changing culture conditions such as those which obtain in our own society. It is even more evident in the case of those who, having begun life in one culture, are attempting to adjust to another. These are the "marginal men" whose plight is recognized by all who have worked with the phenomenon of acculturation. Lacking the reinforcement derived from constant expression in overt behavior, the early-established value-attitude systems of such individuals are weakened and overlaid. At the same time, it seems that they are rarely if ever eliminated, still less replaced by new systems congruous with the cultural milieu in which the individual has to operate. The acculturated individual can learn to act and even to think in terms of his new society's culture, but he cannot learn to feel in these terms. At each point where decision is required he finds himself adrift with no fixed points of reference.

In summary, the fact that personality norms differ for different societies can be explained on the basis of the different experience which the members of such societies acquire from contact with their cultures. In the case of a few small societies whose members have a homogeneous heredity, the influence of physiological factors in determining the psychological potentialities of the majority of these members cannot be ruled out, but the number of such cases is certainly small. Even when common hereditary factors may be present, they can affect only potentialities for response. They are never enough in themselves to account for the differing content and organization which we find in the basic personality types for different societies.

Early in this chapter I cited three conclusions which anthropologists had arrived at as a result of their studies of personality in a wide range of societies and cultures. That personality norms differ for different societies is only the first of these. It is still necessary to explain why the members of any society always show considerable individual variation in personality and also why much the same range of variation and much the same personality types seem to be present in all societies. The first of these problems presents few difficulties. No two individuals, even identical twins, are exactly alike. The members of any society, no matter how closely inbred it may be, differ in their genetically determined potentialities for growth and development. Moreover the working out of these potentialities is affected by all sorts of environmental factors. From the moment of birth on, individuals will differ in size and vigor, while a little later differences in intelligence and learning ability will become apparent. It has already been said that the process of personality formation seems to be mainly one of the integration of experience. This experience, in turn, derives from the interaction of the individual with his environment. It follows that even identical environments, if such things are conceivable, will provide different individuals with different experiences and result in their developing different personalities.

Actually, the situation is much more complicated than this. Even the best-integrated society and culture provides the individuals who are reared in it with environments which are far from uniform. Culture expresses itself to the individual in terms of the behavior of other people and of his contacts with the objects which members of his society habitually make and use. The latter aspect of the cultural environment may be fairly uniform in some of the simpler societies where a combination of general poverty and patterns of sharing prevents the development of marked differences in living standards, but such societies certainly are in the minority. In most communities the various households vary in their equipment and thus provide the children reared in them with somewhat different physical environments. We do not know in how far differences of this sort are significant in personality formation, but everything indicates that they are of rather secondary importance. People have an infinitely greater effect on the developing individual than do things. In particular, the close and continuous contact which the child has with members of his own family, whether parents or siblings, seems to be crucial in establishing his generalized value-attitude systems. Needless to say, the experience which he may derive from such contacts is as varied as the individuals themselves. Even the most rigid culture patterns allow a certain amount of latitude in individual behavior, while the patterns for family relationships can never be too rigid in practice. Someone has said, "Nothing is as continuous as marriage," and the same would apply to parent-child relations. Repeated personal interactions lead to the development of individual patterns of behavior whose range of variation is limited only by fear of what the neighbors may say. Even while acting within the limits imposed by culture, it is possible for parents in any society to be affectionate or indifferent, strict or permissive, sources of aid and security in the child's dealings with outsiders or additional dangers in a generally hostile world. Individual differences and environmental differences can enter into an almost infinite series of permutations and combinations, and the experience which different individuals may derive from these is equally varied. This fact is quite sufficient to account for the differences in personality content which are to be found among the members of any society.

Why much the same range of variation and much the same personality types seem to be present in all societies presents a more difficult problem. Anthropologists themselves are in much less complete agreement on these points than on the preceding ones. Most anthropologists who have had intimate contacts with a number of different societies believe that such is the case, but any real proof or disproof must await the development of much better techniques for personality diagnosis. It must also be understood that when anthropologists say that much the same personality types seem to be present in all societies, in spite of marked differences in their frequencies, the term *personality* is used in a special sense. Most of the specific responses of individuals always fall within the limits set by culture, and it would be too much to expect to find them duplicated in members of different societies. What the anthropologist means is that when one becomes sufficiently familiar with an alien culture and with the individuals who share it, one finds that these individuals are fundamentally the same as various people whom he has known in his own society. While the specific, culturally patterned responses of the two will differ, their abilities and their basic value-attitude systems will be very much the same. This sort of matching does not require any elaborate typing of personalities in technical terms. What it does require is an intimate and sympathetic knowledge of the individuals and cultures involved. One must become exceedingly familiar with the culture of another group before the differences between individual norms of behavior and cultural norms become sufficiently obvious to serve as a guide in judging the deeper levels of individual personalities.

Similarities in the ability levels of members of different societies are not difficult to explain. All human beings are, after all, members of a single species, and the potential range of variations in this respect must be much the same for all societies. Similarities in the generalized value-attitude systems of individuals reared in different cultural environments are more difficult to account for, but there can be no question that they do occur. In the light of our present knowledge the most probable explanation seems to be that they are primarily a result of similar family situations operating upon individuals with similar levels of ability. It has already been noted that culture patterns for the interactions of family members always permit a considerable range of individual variation. In all societies the personalities involved in family situations tend to arrange themselves in much the same orders of dominance and to develop much the same patterns of private, informal interaction. Thus even in the most strongly patriarchal societies one encounters a surprising number of families in which the wife and mother is the dominant member. She may accord her husband exaggerated respect in public, but neither he nor the children will have any doubt as to where real power lies. Again, there are a whole series of biologically conditioned situations which repeat themselves irrespective of the cultural setting. In every society there will be eldest children and youngest children, only children and those reared as members of a large sibling group, feeble, sickly children and strong, vigorous ones. The same thing holds for various sorts of parent-child relationships. There are favorite children, wanted or unwanted children, good sons and black sheep who are constantly subject to suspicion and discipline. Even while operating within the culturally established limits of parental authority, various parents may be affectionate and permissive or take a sadistic delight in exercising their disciplinary functions to the full. Each of these situations will result in a particular sort of early experience for the individual. When essentially similar individuals in different societies are exposed to similar family situations, the result will be a marked similarity in the deeper levels of their personality configurations.

Although the family situations just discussed operate at what might be termed a subcultural level, the frequency with which a particular situation arises in a particular society will be influenced by cultural factors. Thus it is much more difficult for a wife to establish control in a strongly patriarchal society than in a matriarchal one. In the former case she has to work counter to the accepted rules for the marital relationship and to brave all sorts of social pressures. Only a woman of very strong character, or one with a very weak husband, will be able to establish dominance. In the latter case any woman with ordinary strength of character can dominate her household with the aid of social pressures. In every society the bulk of the families will approximate the culturally established norms in their members' interpersonal relationships. It follows that most of the children reared in a particular society will be exposed to similar family situations and will emerge with many elements of even the deeper levels of their personalities in common. This conclusion seems to be borne out by the study of a wide range of societies. In every case numerous correlations can be established between the culture patterns for family organization and child-rearing and the basic personality type for adult members of the society.

In summary, culture must be considered the dominant factor in establishing the basic personality types for various societies and also in establishing the series of status personalities which are characteristic for each society. It must be remembered that basic personality types and status personalities, like culture construct patterns, represent the modes within certain ranges of variation. It is doubtful whether the actual personality of any individual will ever agree at all points with either of these abstractions. With respect to the formation of individual personalities, culture operates as one of a series of factors which also includes the physiologically determined potentialities of the individual and his relations with other individuals. There can be little doubt that in certain cases factors other than the cultural ones are primarily responsible for producing a particular personality configuration. However, it seems that in a majority of cases the cultural factors are dominant. We find that in all societies the personalities of the "average," "normal" individuals who keep the society operating in its accustomed ways can be accounted for in cultural terms. At the same time we find that all societies include atypical individuals whose personalities fall outside the normal range of variation for the society. The causes of such aberrant personalities are still imperfectly understood. They unquestionably derive in part from accidents of early environment and experience. In how far still other, genetically determined factors may be involved we are still unable to say.

In bringing this discussion to a close I am keenly conscious of the number of problems which I have indicated without being able to provide solutions. I am also conscious of the extent to which I have had to depend on techniques which will appear unscientific to those who regard science as something inseparably linked with the laboratory and slide rule. Those who are investigating culture, society and the individual and the complex interrelations of these phenomena are pioneers and, like all pioneers, they have to live by rough and ready methods. They are laboring in the lonely outposts which science has set up on the fringes of a new continent. Even their longest expeditions into the unknown have been mere traverses leaving great unexplored areas between. Those who come after them will be able to draw maps in the terms required by exact science and to exploit riches. The pioneers can only press on, sustained by the belief that somewhere in this vast territory there lies hidden the knowledge which will arm man for his greatest victory, the conquest of himself.

Index

Abilities, inheritance of, 135-136
Adolescents, 67-68
Age-sex categories, 61, 63-68; basis, 66; and culture participation, 64-65; as taxonomic device, 65-66; universal, 66
Anthropological field work, 39-41, 126-127
Associations, 62, 72-73
Attitudes, 111-112

Basic personality type, 129, 131, 136-137, 141-143
Behavior, factors influencing, 10-11; learned, 32-33; organization of, 89; results of, 33-34
Behaviorists, 117

Children, behavior toward, 140; training of, 141-143
Classes, social, 60-61
Communities, 60
Configurations, 2
Culture, configuration, 32; content, 38, 122-123; continuum, 42; covert, 38-39, 41, 123; definition, 32; delimitation through usage, 31-32; differences, 27-28; as environment, 34-35; material, 34; orders of phenomena included, 38; overt, 38, 123; participation in, 55; and personality formation, 47-48, 140; processes, 120-121; real, 43-44, 46; recording of, 39; sampling, 39-40; similarities in, 28-29; study as whole, 29-30; transmission of, 41-42
Culture construct, 43, 45-46; and personality diagnosis, 50-51; and personality formation, 48
Culture patterns, 19-25; as anticipated behavior, 19-20; and experience, 49-50; ideal, 52-53; and personality, 25-26; psychological coherence of, 144; real, 45; shared, 35-37; transmitted, 38
Cultures, 30-31

Data, cultural, collection of, 28
Depth psychology, 118

Emotions, 109-110
Environment, 11, 147
European personality norms, 144
Experience, 11, 132-133

Family, 61, 70-72; behavior within, 71; and culture participation, 70-71; extended, 142-143; influence on members, 142; and personality adjustments, 72; situations within, 149-151; small, 142
Female dominance, 150
Freud, 126

Genetic differences, 137

Habits, 93-94, 106-107
Heredity, 131, 136-137; social, 37-38

Imitation, 96, 140; rewards for, 98
Individual, 5-12; cultural rôle of, 22-23; personality variations, 146-147; socialization of, 18-19; subordination to society, 16-17
Individualization, 13-15
Instincts, human, 14; insect, 12-13
Institutions, 56
Instruction, 24, 97
Intellectual processes, 96

Knowledge, 99-102; false, 100-101; rôle in response, 101-102

Learning, evolution of, 13-14; incentives for, 24-25

Marginal men, 145
Measurements, 2
Methods, experimental, 1-2
Mobility, in England, 61; social, 60-61
Murray thematic apercention tests, 3, 126

Necessities, social, 23-24
Needs, 5-11; functions of, 6, 88-89; intensity of, 89-90; for novelty, 9-10; origins, 8-10; psychic, 6-10; for response, 7-9; for security, 9
Neuroses, 119

Obedience, 142
Occupational groups, 61; behavior ascribed to, 68-69

Personality, 83-124; aberrant, 152; anthropological data on, 126-127; as configuration, 107; content of, 85-86; definition of, 84; and environment, 133-134; functions of, 86; norms, 127-129, 138-146; operation of, 87; organization, 95; and physiological factors, 132-136; processes, 121-122; range of variation, 128; similarities in, 148-149; variations, 127-128
Prestige series, 62, 73-74
Psychoanalysis, 4, 118
Psychological processes, 134-135

Reinforcement, 144
Responses, adjustment of, 103-106; automatized, 106-107; emergent, 93-94, 96, 98-99, 102; established, 93-94, 103-104, 116; extinction of, 114-115; generalized, 108, 111; habitual, 103; overt behavior involved in, 110-111; specific, 107-110
Rewards, social, 92
Rôles, 77-78; conflicting, 80-81; in modern society, 81-82; mutual adjustment of, 80
Romantic love, 143
Rorschach tests, 2, 126, 128

Science of Human Behavior, 4-5
Situation, 87-89; evoking responses, 93; novel, 97; registry of, 87
Social component, 90-92
Social structure, 58-59, 62-63, 74-76; and culture participation, 74-75; and the individual, 75-76

Social systems, 21
Societies, 12-19; anthropoid, 15; division of activities in, 15-17; insect, 12-13; as operative units, 16; organization of, 18, 59-60, 61-62; perpetuation of, 18-21; persistence of, 16; primary, 57-59, 61-62
Society, and culture, 56; definition, 57
Status, 76-78; active, 78; latent, 78
Status personality, 129-131
Stimulus, 88

Tanala, 142
Techniques of research, 4
Tests, psychological, 3
Thinking, 99
Trial and error, 98

Value-attitude systems, 111-114, 129-130; functions of, 112, 114; specificity of, 113

JUL 1 3 2004